SIR WALTER RALEGH Poems selected by RUTH PADEL

Walter Ralegh was born around 1553 in Devon, educated at Oriel
College, Oxford, and fought under Lord Grey in the colonisa-
tion of Ireland, where he met the poet Edmund Spenser, whom
he brought to court in 1598. He sponsored the first colony to
Virginia, sat in Parliament, was knighted, and became Lord
Lieutenant of Cornwall and Captain of the Queen's Guard. In
1592 the Queen discovered his secret marriage and imprisoned
him for a time in the Tower. Later she authorised his expedi-
tion to 'Guiana', now Venezuela, beyond the mouth of the
Orinoco River. Ralegh published an account of this journey
and resumed as Captain of the Guard. When James succeeded
Elizabeth in 1603, Ralegh lost his patents and offices. From 1603
to 1616, he was imprisoned in the Tower, where he wrote and
published *The History of the World*. James released him for
another Guiana expedition but this failed and the 1603 death
sentence was revived. Ralegh was executed in 1618.

Ruth Padel has published seven poetry collections, most recently
*Darwin: A Life in Poems*. Her writing on poetry includes two
books on reading contemporary poems and her Newcastle
Poetry Lectures, *Silent Letters of the Alphabet*. She has written
two books on Greek tragedy, a travel-memoir on tiger conserva-
tion and a novel, *Where the Serpent Lives*. She is a Fellow of the
Royal Society of Literature and Zoological Society of London,
and Bye-Fellow of Christ's College Cambridge.

IN THE POET-TO-POET SERIES

W. H. AUDEN – John Fuller
WILLIAM BARNES – Andrew Motion
JOHN BERRYMAN – Michael Hofmann
JOHN BETJEMAN – Hugo Williams
WILLIAM BLAKE – James Fenton
ROBERT BROWNING – Douglas Dunn
ROBERT BURNS – Don Paterson
LORD BYRON – Paul Muldoon
THOMAS CAMPION – Charles Simic
JOHN CLARE – Paul Farley
SAMUEL TAYLOR COLERIDGE – James Fenton
HART CRANE – Maurice Riordan
EMILY DICKINSON – Ted Hughes
KEITH DOUGLAS – Ted Hughes
JOHN DRYDEN – Charles Tomlinson
ALLEN GINSBERG – Mark Ford
THOM GUNN – August Kleinzahler
THOMAS HARDY – Tom Paulin
GEORGE HERBERT – Jo Shapcott
ROBERT HERRICK – Stephen Romer
A. E. HOUSMAN – Alan Hollinghurst
TED HUGHES – Simon Armitage
BEN JONSON – Thom Gunn
JOHN KEATS – Andrew Motion
D. H. LAWRENCE – Tom Paulin
ROBERT LOWELL – Michael Hofmann
LOUIS MACNEICE – Michael Longley
ANDREW MARVELL – Sean O'Brien
WILFRED OWEN – Jon Stallworthy
SYLVIA PLATH – Ted Hughes
ALEXANDER POPE – John Fuller
EZRA POUND – Thom Gunn
SIR WALTER RALEGH – Ruth Padel
JOHN SKELTON – Anthony Thwaite
JONATHAN SWIFT – Derek Mahon
ALFRED, LORD TENNYSON – Mick Imlah
DYLAN THOMAS – Derek Mahon
WILLIAM WORDSWORTH – Seamus Heaney
THOMAS WYATT – Alice Oswald
W. B. YEATS – Seamus Heaney

# SIR WALTER RALEGH

## Poems selected by RUTH PADEL

*faber and faber*

For Patrick and Mandana, with love

First published in 2010
by Faber and Faber Limited
Bloomsbury House, 74–77 Great Russell Street
London WC1B 3DA

Typeset by RefineCatch Ltd, Bungay, Suffolk
Printed in England by CPI BookMarque, Croydon

A CIP record for this book
is available from the British Library

ISBN 978–0–571–23804–0

10  9  8  7  6  5  4  3  2  1

# Contents

Introduction  ix
Note on the Text  xviii

I  POEMS BY, OR ATTRIBUTED TO,
   SIR WALTER RALEGH
   (*An asterisked poem is one that has been attributed to
   Ralegh but may not be his.*)

1   Nature that Washed Her Hands in Milk  3
2   What Is Our Life? It Is a Play of Passion  5
3   The Lie  6
4   My Broken Pipes Shall on the Willow Hang  9
5   As You Came from the Holy Land*  10
6   The Passionate Man's Pilgrimage*  12
7   Passions Are Likened Best to Floods and Streams*  14
8   The One-and-Twentieth and Last Book of the Ocean to
        Cynthia  15
9   The End of the Books of the Ocean's Love to Cynthia,
        and the Beginning of the Two-and-Twentieth
        Book, Entreating of Sorrow  32
10  A Vision upon this Conceit of *The Faerie Queene*  33
11  Another of the Same  34
12  Farewell to the Court  35
13  Now We Have Present Made  36
14  If Cynthia be a Queen, a Princess and Supreme  38
15  My Body in the Walls Captived  39
16  To the Translator of Lucan  40
17  A Petition to Queen Anne  41
18  A Farewell to False Love  44
19  An Epitaph Upon the Right Honourable Sir Philip
        Sidney, Knight  45
20  Fortune Hath Taken Thee Away, My Love  47
21  The Excuse  48
22  The Nymph's Reply to the Shepherd*  49

23 A Secret Murder Hath Been Done of Late* 50

24 Sought by the World, and Hath the World Disdained* 51

25 What Else is Hell but Loss of Blissful Heaven?* 52

26 On the Cards and the Dice* 53

27 Sweet Are the Thoughts where Hope Persuadeth Hap* 54

28 A Poesy to Prove Affection Is not Love* 55

29 A Poem Put into My Lady Leighton's Pocket* 57

30 Feed Still Thyself, Thou Fondling, with Belief* 58

31 Like to a Hermit Poor in Place Obscure* 59

32 My First-Born Love, Unhappily Conceived* 60

33 The Advice* 61

34 Sir Walter Ralegh to His Son* 62

35 An Epigram on Henry Noel 63

36 Sir W. Ralegh on the Snuff of a Candle the Night before He Died* 64

37 De Morte* 65

38 In Commendation of *The Steel Glass* 66

39 Verse Translations from *The History of the World* 67

40 Even Such is Time, Which Takes in Trust 78

II EXCHANGES AND RIPOSTES: POEMS BY QUEEN ELIZABETH, BEN JONSON, CHRISTOPHER MARLOWE, PHILIP SIDNEY, EDMUND SPENSER AND OTHERS

41 EDMUND SPENSER: To the Right Noble and Valorous Knight, Sir Walter Ralegh 81

42 CHRISTOPHER MARLOWE: The Passionate Shepherd to His Love 82

43 QUEEN ELIZABETH: On Monsieur's Departure 83

44 Ah Silly Pug, Wert Thou so Sore Afraid? 84

45 A Hapless Kind of Life Is This I Wear 85

46 The Doubt of Future Foes Exiles My Present Joy 86

47 Now Leave and Let Me Rest 87

48 ROBERT DEVEREUX, EARL OF ESSEX: Change Thy Mind since She Doth Change 89

49 Go, Echo of the Mind, a Careless Truth Protest 90

| 50 | When Wert Thou Born, Desire? 92 |
| 51 | Seated between the Old World and the New 93 |
| 52 | To Plead My Faith where Faith Hath No Reward 94 |
| 53 | Happy Were He Could Finish Forth His Fate 95 |
| 54 | Verses Made by the Earl of Essex in His Trouble 96 |
| 55 | I Am Not as I Seem, I Seem and Am the Same 97 |
| 56 | EDWARD DE VERE, EARL OF OXFORD: I Am Not as I Seem to Be 98 |
| 57 | The Lively Lark Stretched Forth Her Wing 100 |
| 58 | SIR EDWARD DYER: The Shepherd's Conceit of Prometheus 101 |
| 59 | SIR PHILIP SIDNEY: A Reply 102 |
| 60 | HENRY NOEL: The Foe to the Stomach and the Word of Disgrace 103 |
| 61 | UNKNOWN: If Breath Were Made for Every Man to Buy 104 |
| 62 | SIR THOMAS HENEAGE: Most Welcome Love, Thou Mortal Foe to Lies 105 |
| 63 | Madam, but Mark the Labours of Our Life 106 |
| 64 | SIR HENRY LEE: Sir Henry Lee's Farewell to the Court 107 |
| 65 | Far from Triumphing Court and Wonted Glory 108 |
| 66 | SIR HENRY WOTTON: The Character of a Happy Life 109 |
| 67 | On His Mistress, the Queen of Bohemia 110 |
| 68 | Upon the Sudden Restraint of the Earl of Somerset, then Falling from Favour 111 |
| 69 | This Hymn 112 |
| 70 | BEN JONSON: The Mind of the Frontispiece to Ralegh's *History of the World* 114 |

The Poets 115

# Introduction

Walter Ralegh, courtier, soldier, explorer and travel writer, captivated a nation. Low-born but high-playing, this glamorous 'great Lucifer' beguiled, amused and sometimes infuriated a queen. But after Elizabeth died, Ralegh paid dearly for his charisma. He was forty-nine when James I locked him in the Tower. For over a decade, people came and gazed at the celebrity prisoner strolling the ramparts. Finally, at sixty-two, he was executed. No one really knows why James was so against him, but his rise and fall made him a perfect emblem of the human condition for that tragedy-conscious age.

But he was a poet, too. In the first half of this book are poems by him, or poems people believed were his. Some of them are among the best-loved poems of Elizabeth's day. Poems like 'As You Came from the Holy Land' and 'The Passionate Man's Pilgrimage' (Nos 5 and 6) may not in fact be by Ralegh, but the vivid, ballad-like drama in them, the urgent relation to the reader, the music, rich imagery, loneliness, passion, wit and faith, tell us what qualities people associated with Ralegh, and point to his perceived identity as poet as well as man.

Rather than suggesting a chronology, I have arranged the poems in a way which I hope lets them speak to each other. We begin with 'Nature that Washed her Hands in Milk' because I love the surprise and cheek of that first image, and the quick movement of feeling all through. It seems to me to encapsulate his energy. It is a love poem and we know Ralegh risked his career by marrying secretly the Queen's lady-in-waiting, Bess Throckmorton. Five years later the Queen found out and sent them both, for a while, to the Tower. Did Ralegh write this poem for his beloved wife? At one level it doesn't matter. A good love poem may be words for a particular person, but like all good poems they are also self-delighting, words playing with love in such a way as to renew the reader's own experience. Still, this poem meant a lot to Ralegh for before his death he reworked its last stanza into the poem of religious faith, No. 40, which I have put at the end of his own section.

Except for the mysterious Ocean fragments, Nos 8 and 9, the poems in between shimmer with wit, control, quick grace, imagination, vitality and vivid confidence. Ralegh loves the weight and echo of words. Succeeding lines echo each other's interiors ('In vain, mine eyes, in vain you waste your tears./ In vain, my sighs, the smokes of my despaires'). Words see-saw against and balance each other in the centre of a line. 'Then had my love my love for ever been.' 'Her eyes he would should be of light.' 'I loved myself because myself loved you.' The symmetry of that line makes it a perfect V. 'Because', at the centre at the bottom, joins 'I' at the beginning to 'you' at the end. 'Loved myself' and 'myself loved' make a self-ironic mirror between.

He does this all deceptively lightly but the stakes were high and behind every word is an obsessingly precarious relationship to an all-important *you*. Not his wife, but the Queen. Today's poets write to Arts Councils, universities and the media, chasing grants, salaries, reviews. Elizabeth's poets, in a finely calibrated game of snakes-and-ladders, courted a capricious and skilled political mistress, a highly intelligent but easily affronted single woman.

The ladders led to estates, appointments, monopolies – Ralegh made his fortune by courting Elizabeth and his first wealth came from a patent to export broadcloth – but snakes led to the Tower, to the executioner's block. And so all poetry at her court had a high-tensile political dimension, a lethal echo-chamber. The heady, dangerous relationship with the Queen, and the poet's sense of these dangers, convert Ralegh's images of joy and light to night, death and loss. These are poems written by someone living on, and imagining on, a knife edge between eroticism, *politesse*, ambition and despair.

Ralegh came from impoverished gentry and began with nothing but his natural gifts. Born around 1553 in a house near Exmouth which is still a working farmhouse, he 'spoke broad Devonshire all his life', though he also knew Spanish, French and probably Italian. The many stories about his real-life relations with the Queen suggest intelligent intimacy enjoyed by both for years. When she bet him that he could not weigh smoke, he weighed some tobacco, smoked it, then weighed the ash and said the difference between the weight of tobacco and ash was the weight of the smoke. Paying up, she said she'd heard of men who turned gold into smoke but he was the first to turn smoke into gold.

But in 1584, when he was over thirty, a magnetic and ultra-aristocratic teenager appeared at court. The Earl of Essex was fifteen years younger and powerfully connected. By 1587, when Elizabeth desperately needed a new distraction because Parliament was forcing her to sign Mary's death warrant, Essex became Ralegh's serious rival for the Queen's attention. Poem No. 21 is supposedly Ralegh's response. Ralegh had no network of powerful connections behind him. He depended entirely on his relationship with the Queen. Worse, when he was over forty, she imprisoned him in the Tower for marrying. He did bounce back but it was increasingly hard to keep his feet against rivals.

Poetically, though, out of this all-important relationship with Elizabeth, Ralegh created a chivalrous tonality which, rather than turning smoke to gold, turned the feverish, super-sophisticated sexuality of that court to an almost post-modernly ironic reverence. 'I found myself the cause of all my smart./ And told myself, Myself to slay I will./ Yet when I saw myself to you was true,/ I loved myself, because myself loved you.'

But I feel there is another passionate relationship behind his poetry, with something less fickle: the Latin language. Ralegh was a passionate scholar. He took books with him everywhere on his travels and also to the Tower, where he wrote a *History of the World* threaded with his own verse translations from ancient poems – such as No. 39 – which breathe his sensitivity to the original Latin. From Catullus, for instance. 'The sun may set and rise/ But we, contrariwise/ Sleep after our short light/ One everlasting night.' You hear in these lines a deep love for the original, as well as the pleasure of rising to a verbal challenge.

Classical Latin poetry revels in symmetry, and I think is a driving inspiration behind Ralegh's own gift.

Poem No. 5, 'As You Came from the Holy Land', is a version of a famous English song, the Walsingham Ballad. The original conjured a pilgrim journey to the Virgin's shrine. Later versions changed this to a quest for a lost girlfriend. In *Hamlet*, Shakespeare changed the sexes: in Ophelia's song it is a girl who has lost her lover, a pilgrim with a cockle hat, staff and 'sandal shoon'.

Whether No. 5 was really by Ralegh or not, it suggests three themes which popular imagination connected with him as a poet. The first is 'sorrow', one of the commonest nouns in Ralegh's poems. Melancholy was a favourite Elizabethan pose but comes to Ralegh's pen suspiciously easily. 'Love likes not the falling fruit/ From the withered tree': you get a sense of how tense and self-suspicious this poet is, how aware of his own precariousness. Life is a walk along a crust of barely cooled lava: he might fall in at any moment. You feel the shining words might crackle and darken like taffeta if you touched them. The flip side of success is a total blackness. The second theme is the journey, which powers No. 6, too, 'The Passionate Man's Pilgrimage', supposedly written the night before Ralegh was due to be executed. I shall come back to Ralegh's public association not only with pilgrimage but also with sea journeys, like his voyage to Guiana undertaken for another Virgin, the Queen.

Thirdly, erotic love. Aubrey, in his *Brief Lives*, says Ralegh 'loved a wench well' but there is no contemporary evidence for wenching as there is for him risking his career for his wife. Yet all his poetry is, in a way, a form of dangerous courtship and one of its hallmarks is passion.

Life as well as poetry at court turned on a constant response to other people, and so the second half of this book is poems by other people: by Ralegh's friends and rivals. It Includes poems by Elizabeth, who had to keep control of her courtful of poetically competing males. Poetry was part of her armoury as well as theirs: they were all at it. One story about Ralegh and

Elizabeth says it all. 'Fain would I climb, yet fear I to fall,' he sup-posedly wrote on a glass window. (What with, one wonders.) The Queen replied beneath, 'If thy heart fails thee, climb not at all.' Whatever tool Ralegh was using on the glass, she had one too. Her reply commands, addresses, hints at possible rewards but caps his line by rhyming it, reminding him who's boss.

The poets in this second half of the selection worked in very different ways and their poems served different functions. Diehard court poets did not usually publish their poems. A court poem had other things to do than get read by the pub-lic. It was social self-assertion, a means of showing off. Court poetry was an answering game and there were no innocent readers. Poems were bejewelled statements aimed at someone else, often packaged in the dative (grammatically, the 'giving' case, denoting 'to' and 'for'; 'to' is all over the Contents list). Titles were often vocative – the 'calling on' or 'addressing' case. 'Madam, but Mark the Labours of Our Life'. Many are in imper-ative mode. 'Now Leave and Let Me Rest'. Men wrote poems 'for' the Queen and 'to' each other. The driving force was wit. As in No. 35, answered by No. 60.

Many poems of this second half are 'reply poems'. Some reply to Ralegh. Several men wrote jealous poems in answer to his poem 'The Lie' (No. 3). No. 49 may be Essex responding to something personal and direct from Ralegh with a stream of patronising artifice. Sometimes Ralegh's poem is the answer, as in No. 21. In No. 44, the Queen gives an elegantly reassur-ing reply. Despite her new attachment to Essex, she does like Ralegh, really. No. 23, though, is a reply to one of the loveliest of English love poems, No. 42. Whether 23 is by Ralegh or not, it reflects the way that all of Ralegh's writing, prose and poetry, lives not only off rich imagery but also off immediate physical detail. This is true of his travel writing too. 'We stayed awhile to dry our shirts, which with the heat hung very wet and heavy on our shoulders,' he writes in *The Discovery of Guyana*.

These are mainly court poems but we should remember their violent context. Their poets knew how to kill. There are thirteen of them here, twelve men and one woman. Only three or four were not physically responsible for deaths of other people. Four, including Ralegh, died by the sword or the axe. War was part of a gentleman's education. Ralegh was very good at it, meaning ruthless. He first saw battle at the age of fifteen, in France. As captain for Lord Grey, colonising Ireland, he helped capture the town of Smerwick. The English agreed an unconditional surrender but then launched into a massacre which horrified Europe. To keep your sword sharp, recommended massacre technique was a light stroke to the neck or jab in the belly, which also ensured lingering death. As Seamus Heaney remembers in his poem 'Ocean's Love to Ireland', Ralegh and his colleagues worked their way like this through six hundred terrified men.

Between 1580 and 1590, Ralegh acquired vast lands in Ireland and killed thousands of people. Yet he later wrote, 'The miseries of war are never so many and bitter as when a whole nation, or great part of it, forsaking their own seats, labour to root out the established possessors of another land.' It is as if Robert Lowell fought in Vietnam, led the My Lai massacre and then, from a luxury villa bought on his war profits, wrote eloquently on the sufferings of South East Asia.

Ralegh fought as a soldier but reflected on his actions as a historian and a poet. The ability to separate the two was encouraged by the age, and particularly by the court. The poets here who are major figures in English literature today did not live at court. Sidney is the only aristocrat. Spenser did not make it as a courtier. (Urged by Ralegh, the Queen appointed Spenser Poet Laureate, but he died in penury.) Professional poets were not soldiers but entertainers: in music, like Campion, or theatre like Marlowe and Shakespeare. Ben Jonson, twenty years younger than Ralegh, began as a not-very-good actor, then fell into writing plays. Of the poets here, only Jonson and Marlowe lived by the pen.

Ralegh was a court poet but kept a strong sense of where he came from and what lay at his heart. He settled in the place he came from, the West Country. He wanted to buy the house at Hayes Barton where he was born, where he lived till he was twelve. When I went to look at it, the family which lives there showed me a photocopy of the letter he wrote, trying (and failing) to buy it. 'For the natural disposition I have to that place being borne in that house,' he explains in a small flowing hand that seems to love the act of writing, 'I had rather seat myself there than anywhere else.'

His wife, I think, was the centre of his emotional life. 'You shall now receive (my deare wife) my last words in these last lines,' he wrote to her before he died. 'My love I send you that you may keep it when I am dead. I would not by my will present you with sorrowes (dear Besse) let them go to the grave with me and be buried in the dust. And seeing that it is not Gods will that I should see you any more in this life, beare it patiently, and with a heart like thy selfe.' But poetry was his centre too. And here the person who most mattered was another poet, Edmund Spenser. The reply poems that bring us closest to Ralegh as a poet, when he is thinking about poetry in itself rather than as a tool, are Nos 10 and 11, commending *The Faerie Queene*. From the literary point of view, the most important thing Ralegh did in Ireland, one of the wildest parts of Elizabeth's empire, was listen, and read his own work, to Edmund Spenser. Ralegh's estate was near Spenser's: Elizabeth wanted to keep them both on that island. Through the 1580s Ralegh had the chance to talk poetry properly, away from court where poetry was a weapon, and to think about poetry as it was, or could be, with someone who was giving his life to it. Ralegh recognised *The Faerie Queene*'s greatness; Spenser generously admired Ralegh's 'lofty Muse' (No. 41). In *Colin Clout's Come Home Again* (printed 1595, inscribed to Ralegh in 1591), Spenser depicted them both as shepherds 'piping' to each other in turn.

Spenser also addresses Ralegh as 'shepheard of the Ocean', which brings us back to that image of the journey. Spenser was responding to Ralegh's sea expeditions but also, perhaps, to the way Ralegh's images and allusions are fired by visions of elsewhere.

Ralegh's imagination was characteristically Elizabethan, based on the elsewhere, but his energy and ambition took his body where his mind and metaphors had gone. When he writes (No. 13), 'She is that valley in Peru/ Whose summer ever lasteth,' the foreign name has a weight it might not have from a poet using Peru as easy exoticism.

Above all, though, Spenser was responding to Ralegh's most ambitious poetic project, 'The Ocean's Love to Cynthia'. This work is a mystery. All we have are the two fragments, Nos 8 and 9. No one knows when Ralegh wrote them. It must have been before Elizabeth died. Was there any more of this work? Again, no one knows. There is only this; and only one manuscript of it. Ralegh's 'Ocean' poems divide critics. Some find the poetry sterile, others say it is Ralegh's loveliest work and shows what a poet he could have been if he had not wasted his time colonising the Americas and fighting Armadas. I guess that when Spenser read him *The Faerie Queene*, and Ralegh encountered for the first time a truly original large-scale poem, he did what any poet would do – thought, Can I do something like that? When he saw 'Homer's sprite' trembling at Spenser's poem (No. 10), he dreamed of writing an epic himself: of finding a new poetic identity. He had lived by risk but had not written out of risk. Writing court poems, he risked things personally but not poetically; he was merely doing brilliantly what he knew he could do well. Now he hit on a new writing persona: Ocean, something enormous, something you cannot rely on but which takes you to new worlds. As for the all-important 'you' in his head, the Queen, that was easy: the virgin goddess, Diana or Cynthia, was also goddess of the moon who ruled the sea. 'We should begin by such a parting light/ To write the story of all ages past/ And end the same before the approaching night.'

In the generous sense of forwarding the craft which often grows between poets sharing their work, this idea would have excited Spenser too. All poets are interested in new ways of doing things. Both, in very different ways, were trying to write great poetry on a large scale, to honour the same Queen. But then Ralegh's relation to the Queen turned to nightmare. In 1592, while Ralegh was (I imagine) still considering his epic, Elizabeth discovered his marriage and sent him to the Tower. His dream became catastrophe, the grandeur became grand self-pity. What came out was a kaleidoscopic howl with no clear movement. Formless poetry, from a poet who had always kept control. 'To seek new worlds for gold, for praise, for glory,/ To try desire, to try love sever'd far,/ When I was gone, she sent her memory,/ More strong than were ten thousand ships of war.'

Long after, when Elizabeth was dead, Ralegh petitioned Queen Anne in a poem (No. 17) which re-used the first two stanzas of No. 9, then skipped to the words where No. 9 broke off and developed them. In a poem with a purpose, like asking another queen for help, he *could* refind control and structure. But the 'Ocean' poems themselves seethe like stormy sea, with rich chaotic imagery, irregular metre, fluctuating stanza lengths. Incompleteness is their heart.

Maybe that was the point. Maybe Ralegh wanted to show to what tatters the moon who ruled his personal sea had reduced him. The poem is in bits, like himself. It is, like himself, a thing that could have been.

I like to think he never wrote the twenty other books and these fragments are a Borges-like fiction, wildly ahead of its time. But they may be the poetic equivalent of the lost colony he sent to North Carolina, remnants from an experiment which did not work.

Ralegh's 'Ocean' poetry is all over the place. But so is ocean. And so, physically and emotionally, was Ralegh too. A tireless traveller, determined, mercurial, full of curiosity, he was passionate in everything he did. 'What is our life?' he says in No. 2. 'A play of passion', the 'Ocean' fragments are unique in his work because they are passion without play. But they are the exception that proves the rule. In his other poems what you get is play and passion both.

RUTH PADEL

## Note on the Text

For the sake of immediacy, I have kept to modern spellings. The texts I have used are those of Martin Dodsworth in *Sir Walter Ralegh* (Everyman's Poetry, J. M. Dent, 1999), and J. Hannah in *The Poems of Sir Walter Raleigh, Collected and Authenticated, with those of Sir Hentry Wotton and Other Courtly Poets from 1540 1650* (George Bell and Sons, 1892).

# I POEMS BY, OR ATTRIBUTED TO, SIR WALTER RALEGH

# 1 Nature that Washed Her Hands in Milk

Nature, that washed her hands in milk
    And had forgot to dry them,
Instead of earth took snow and silk
    At Love's request, to try them
If she a mistress could compose
To please Love's fancy out of those.

Her eyes he would should be of light,
    A violet breath and lips of jelly,
Her hair not black nor over-bright,
    And of the softest down her belly;
As for her inside he'd have it
Only of wantonness and wit.

At Love's entreaty, such a one
    Hath Nature made, but with her beauty
She hath framed a heart of stone,
    So as Love by his ill destiny
Must die for her whom Nature gave him
Because her darling would not save him.

But Time, which Nature doth despise
    And rudely gives her love the lie,
Makes Hope a fool, Sorrow wise,
    His hands doth neither wash nor dry
But, being made of steel and rust,
Turns snow and silk and milk to dust.

The light, the belly, lips and breath,
    He dims, discolours and destroys;
With those he feeds but fills not Death,
    Which sometime were the food of joys.
Yea, Time doth dull each lively wit
And dries all wantonness with it.

O cruel Time, which takes in trust
        Our youth, our joys and all we have,
And pays us but with age and dust,
        Who in the dark and silent grave
When we have wandered all our ways
Shuts up the story of our days.

## 2 What Is Our Life? It Is a Play of Passion

What is our life? It is a play of passion.
What is our mirth? The music of division.
Our mothers, they the tiring-houses be,
Where we are dressed for time's short tragedy.
Earth is the stage, heaven the spectator is
Who doth behold whoever doth act amiss.
The graves that hide us from the parching sun
Are but drawn curtains till the play is done.

## 3 The Lie

[Answered by No. 49]

Go soul, the body's guest,
Upon a thankless arrant,
Fear not to touch the best,
The truth shall be thy warrant.
      Go, since I needs must die,
      And give the world the lie.

Say to the Court, it glows
And shines like rotten wood,
Say to the Church, it shows
What's good, but doth no good:
      If Church and Court reply,
      Give Court and Church the lie.

Tell potentates, they live
Acting by others' actions,
Not loved unless they give,
Not strong but by affections:
      If potentates reply,
      Give potentates the lie.

Tell men of high condition,
That in affairs of state
Their purpose is ambition,
Their practice only hate,
      And if they once reply,
      Then give them all the lie.

Tell them that brave it most,
They beg for more by spending,
Who, in their greatest cost,
Seek nothing but commending:
    And if they make reply,
      Give each of them the lie.

Tell zeal it wants devotion,
Tell love it is but lust.
Tell time it metes but motion,
Tell flesh it is but dust.
    And wish them not reply,
      For thou must give the lie.

Tell age it daily wasteth,
Tell honour how it alters.
Tell beauty that she blasteth,
Tell favour how it falters.
    And as they shall reply
      Give every one the lie.

Tell wit how much it wrangles
In tickle points of niceness,
Tell wisdom she entangles
Herself in over-wiseness.
    And when they do reply
      Straight give them both the lie.

Tell physic of her boldness,
Tell skill it is prevention,
Tell charity of coldness,
Tell law it is contention.
    And as they do reply
      So give them still the lie.

Tell Fortune of her blindness,
Tell nature of decay,
Tell friendship of unkindness.
Tell justice of delay.
    And if they will reply.
    Then give them all the lie.

Tell arts they have no soundness,
But vary by esteeming;
Tell schools they want profoundness,
And stand too much on seeming.
    If arts and schools reply,
    Give arts and schools the lie.

Tell faith it's fled the city,
Tell how the country erreth,
Tell manhood shakes off pity
And virtue least preferreth.
    And if they do reply,
    Spare not to give the lie.

So when thou hast, as I
Commanded thee, done blabbing,
Although to give the lie
Deserves no less than stabbing,
    Stab at thee he that will,
    No stab the soul can kill.

## 4 My Broken Pipes Shall on the Willow Hang

My broken pipes shall on the willow hang,
Like those which on the Babylonian banks,
Their joys foredone, their present sorrow sang
– These times to worth yielding but frozen thanks.

## 5  As You Came from the Holy Land*

As you came from the holy land
    Of Walsingham,
Met you not with my true love
    By the way as you came?

How shall I know your true love,
    That have met many one,
As I went to the holy land,
    That have come, that have gone?

She is neither white nor brown,
    But as the heavens fair;
There is none hath a form so divine
    In the earth or the air.

Such an one did I meet, good sir,
    Such an angelic face,
Who like a queen, like a nymph, did appear,
    By her gait, by her grace.

She hath left me here all alone,
    All alone, as unknown,
Who sometimes did me lead with herself,
    And me loved as her own.

What's the cause that she leaves you alone
    And a new way doth take,
Who lov'd you once as her own,
    And her joy did you make?

I have loved her all my youth,
    But now old, as you see.
Love likes not the falling fruit
    From the withered tree.

Know that Love is a careless child,
    And forgets promise past;
He is blind, he is deaf when he list,
    And in faith never fast.

His desire is a dureless content,
    And a trustless joy;
He is won with a world of despair,
    And is lost with a toy.

Of womenkind such indeed is the love,
    Or the word 'love' abused,
Under which many childish desires
    And conceits are excused.

But true love is a durable fire,
    In the mind ever burning,
Never sick, never old, never dead,
    From itself never turning.

## 6 The Passionate Man's Pilgrimage*

Give me my scallop shell of quiet,
My staff of faith to walk upon,
My scrip of joy, immortal diet,
My bottle of salvation,
My gown of glory, hope's true gage,
And thus I'll take my pilgrimage.

Blood must be my body's balmer,
No other balm will there be given,
Whilst my soul, like quiet palmer,
Travelleth towards the land of heaven
Over the silver mountains,
Where spring the nectar fountains.
There will I kiss
The bowl of bliss,
And drink my eternal fill
On every milken hill.
My soul will be adry before,
But after, it will thirst no more.

Then by the happy blissful way
More peaceful pilgrims I shall see,
That have cast off their rags of clay,
And go apparelled fresh like me.
I'll bring them first
To quench their thirst
And then to taste of nectar suckets,
At the clear wells
Where sweetness dwells,
Drawn up by saints in crystal buckets.

And when our bottles and all we
Are filled with immortality,
Then the holy paths we'll travel,
Strewed with rubies thick as gravel;
Ceilings of diamonds, sapphire floors,
High walls of coral, pearl bowers.
From thence to heaven's bribeless hall,
Where no corrupted voices brawl,
No conscience molten into gold,
No forged accuser bought and sold,
No cause deferred, no vain-spent journey,
For there Christ is the King's Attorney,
Who pleads for all without degrees,
And he hath angels, but no fees.
And when the grand twelve-million jury
Of our sins with direful fury
Against our souls black verdicts give,
Christ pleads His death, and then we live.
Be Thou my speaker, taintless pleader,
Unblotted lawyer, true proceeder;
Thou movest salvation even for alms,
Not with a bribed lawyer's palms.

And this is mine eternal plea
To him that made heaven, earth, and sea,
Seeing my flesh must die so soon,
And want a head to dine next noon,
Just at the stroke, when my veins start and spread,
Set on my soul an everlasting head.
Then am I ready, like a palmer fit,
To tread those blest paths which before I writ.

## 7 Passions Are Likened Best to Floods and Streams*

Passions are likened best to floods and streams;
The shallow murmur, but the deep are dumb.
So when affection yields discourse, it seems
The bottom is but shallow whence they come.
    They that are rich in words, in words discover
    That they are poor in that which makes a lover.

# 8  The One-and-Twentieth and Last Book of the Ocean to Cynthia

Sufficeth it to you, my joys interred,
In simple words that I my woes complain;
You that then died when first my fancy erred,
Joys under dust that never live again.

If to the living were my muse addressed,
Or did my mind her own spirit still inhold,
Were not my living passion so repressed
As to the dead the dead did these unfold,

Some sweeter words, some more becoming verse
Should witness my mishap in higher kind;
But my love's wounds, my fancy in the hearse,
The idea but resting of a wasted mind,

The blossoms fallen, the sap gone from the tree,
The broken monuments of my great desires,
From these so lost what may the affections be?
What heat in cinders of extinguished fires?

Lost in the mud of those high-flowing streams,
Which through more fairer fields their courses bend,
Slain with self-thoughts, amazed in fearful dreams,
Woes without date, discomforts without end:

From fruitful trees I gather withered leaves.
And glean the broken ears with miser's hand,
Who sometime did enjoy the weighty sheaves:
I seek fair flowers amid the brinish sand.

All in the shade, even in the fair sun days,
Under those healthless trees I sit alone,
Where joyful birds sing neither lovely lays,
Nor Philomen recounts her direful moan.

No feeding flocks, no shepherd's company,
That might renew my dolorous conceit,
While happy then, while love and fantasy
Confined my thoughts on that fair flock to wait;

No pleasing streams fast to the ocean wending,
The messengers sometimes of my great woe;
But all on earth, as from the cold storms bending,
Shrink from my thoughts in high heavens or below.

O hopeful love, my object and invention,
O true desire, the spur of my conceit,
O worthiest spirit, my mind's impulsion,
O eyes transpersant, my affection's bait,

Oh, princely form, my fancy's adamant,
Divine conceit, my pains' acceptance,
O all in one! O heaven on earth transparent!
The seat of joys and love's abundance!

Out of that mass of miracles, my muse
Gathered those flowers, to her pure senses pleasing;
Out of her eyes, the store of joys, did choose
Equal delights, my sorrows counterpoising.

Her regal looks my vigorous sighs suppressed;
Small drops of joys sweetened great worlds of woes;
One gladsome day a thousand cares redressed;
Whom love defends, what fortune overthrows?

When she did well, what did there else amiss?
When she did ill, what empires would have pleased?
No other power effecting woe or bliss,
She gave, she took, she wounded, she appeased.

The honour of her love Love still devising,
Wounding my mind with contrary conceit,
Transferred itself sometime to her aspiring,
Sometime the trumpet of her thought's retreat.

To seek new worlds for gold, for praise, for glory,
To try desire, to try love severed far,
When I was gone, she sent her memory,
More strong than were ten thousand ships of war.

To call me back, to leave great honour's thought,
To leave my friends, my fortune, my attempt;
To leave the purpose I so long had sought,
And hold both cares and comforts in contempt.

Such heat in ice, such fire in frost remained,
Such trust in doubt, such comfort in despair,
Much like the gentle lamb, though lately weaned,
Plays with the dug, though finds no comfort there.

But as a body, violently slain,
Retaineth warmth although the spirit be gone,
And by a power in nature moves again
Till it be laid below the fatal stone;

Or as the earth, even in cold winter days,
Left for a time by her life-giving sun,
Doth by the power remaining of his rays
Produce some green, though not as it hath done;

Or as a wheel, forced by the falling stream,
Although the course be turned some other way,
Doth for a time go round upon the beam,
Till, wanting strength to move, it stands at stay;

So my forsaken heart, my withered mind,
Widow of all the joys it once possessed,
My hopes clean out of sight with forced wind
To kingdoms strange, to lands far-off addressed,

Alone, forsaken, friendless, on the shore
With many wounds, with death's cold pangs embraced,
Writes in the dust, as one that could no more,
Whom love, and time, and fortune, had defaced,

Of things so great, so long, so manifold,
With means so weak, the soul even then departing,
The weal, the woe, the passages of old,
And worlds of thoughts described by one last sighing,

As if, when after Phoebus is descended,
And leaves a light much like the past day's dawning,
And, every toil and labour wholly ended,
Each living creature draweth to his resting,

We should begin by such a parting light
To write the story of all ages past,
And end the same before the approaching night.

Such is again the labour of my mind,
Whose shroud, by sorrow woven now to end,
Hath seen that ever shining sun declined,
So many years that so could not descend,

But that the eyes of my mind held her beams
In every part transferred by love's swift thought
Far off or near, in waking or in dreams;
Imagination strong their lustre brought,

Such force her angelic appearance had
To master distance, time, or cruelty;
Such art to grieve, and after to make glad;
Such fear in love, such love in majesty.

My weary limbs her memory embalmed;
My darkest ways her eyes make clear as day.
What storms so great but Cynthia's beams appeased?
What rage so fierce that love could not allay?

Twelve years entire I wasted in this war,
Twelve years of my most happy younger days;
But I in them, and they now wasted are,
'Of all which past, the sorrow only stays.'

So wrate I once, and my mishap foretold,
My mind still feeling sorrowful success,
Even as before a storm the marble cold
Doth by moist tears tempestuous times express.

So felt my heavy mind my harms at hand,
Which my vain thought in vain sought to recure:
At middle day my sun seemed under land,
When any little cloud did it obscure.

And as the icicles in a winter's day,
Whenas the sun shines with unwonted warm,

So did my joys melt into secret tears;
So did my heart dissolve in wasting drops:
And as the season of the year outwears,
And heaps of snow from off the mountain tops

With sudden streams the valleys overflow,
So did the time draw on my more despair:
Then floods of sorrow and whole seas of woe
The banks of all my hope did overbear,

And drowned my mind in depths of misery.
Sometime I died; sometime I was distract,
My soul the stage of fancy's tragedy:
Then furious madness, where true reason lacked,

Wrate what it would, and scourged mine own conceit.
O heavy heart! who can thee witness bear?
What tongue, what pen, could thy tormenting treat,
But thine own mourning thoughts which present were?

What stranger mind believe the meanest part?
What altered sense conceive the weakest woe,
That tare, that rent, that pierced thy sad heart?

And as a man distract, with treble might,
Bound in strong chains, doth strive and rage in vain,
Till, tired and breathless, he is forced to rest,
Finds by contention but increase of pain,
And fiery heat inflamed in swollen breast;

So did my mind in change of passion
From woe to wrath, from wrath return to woe,
Struggling in vain from love's subjection.

Therefore, all lifeless and all helpless bound,
My fainting spirits sunk, and heart appalled,
My joys and hopes lay bleeding on the ground,
That not long since the highest heaven scaled.

I hated life and cursed destiny;
The thoughts of passed times, like flames of hell,
Kindled afresh within my memory
The many dear achievements that befell

In those prime years and infancy of love,
Which to describe were but to die in writing;
Ah, those I sought, but vainly, to remove,
And vainly shall, by which I perish living.

And though strong reason hold before mine eyes
The images and forms of worlds past,
Teaching the cause why all those flames that rise
From forms external can no longer last,

Than that those seeming beauties hold in prime,
Love's ground, his essence, and his empery,
All slaves to age, and vassals unto time,
Of which repentance writes the tragedy,

But this my heart's desire could not conceive,
Whose love outflew the fastest flying time,
A beauty that can easily deceive
The arrest of years, and creeping age outclimb,

A spring of beauties which time ripeth not
(Time that but works on frail mortality);
A sweetness which woe's wrongs outwipeth not,
Whom love hath chose for his divinity;

A vestal fire that burns but never wasteth,
That loseth nought by giving light to all,
That endless shines eachwhere, and endless lasteth,
Blossoms of pride that can nor fade nor fall.

These were those marvellous perfections,
The parents of my sorrow and my envy,
Most deathful and most violent infections;
These be the tyrants that in fetters tie

Their wounded vassals, yet nor kill nor cure,
But glory in their lasting misery;
That, as her beauties, would our woes should dure.
These be the effects of powerful empery . . .

Yet have these wonders want, which want compassion;
Yet hath her mind some marks of human race;
Yet will she be a woman for a fashion,
So doth she please her virtues to deface.

And like as that immortal power doth seat
An element of waters, to allay
The fiery sunbeams that on earth do beat
And temper by cold night the heat of day,

So hath perfection, which begat her mind,
Added thereto a change of fantasy,
And left her the affections of her kind,
Yet free from every evil but cruelty.

But leave her praise; speak thou of nought but woe:
Write on the tale that Sorrow bids thee tell;
Strive to forget, and care no more to know
Thy cares are known, by knowing those too well.

Describe her now as she appears to thee,
Not as she did appear in days fordone.
In love, those things that were no more may be,
For fancy seldom ends where it begun.

And as a stream by strong hand bounded in,
From nature's course where it did sometime run
By some small rent or loose part doth begin
To find escape, till it a way hath won;

Doth then all unawares in sunder tear
The forced bounds, and, raging, run at large
In the ancient channels as they wonted were;
Such is of women's love the careful charge,

Held and maintained with multitude of woes;
Of long erections such the sudden fall.
One hour diverts, one instant overthrows,
For which our lives, for which our fortune's thrall

So many years those joys have dearly bought;
Of which when our fond hopes do most assure,
All is dissolved; our labours come to nought,
Nor any mark thereof there doth endure:

No more than when small drops of rain do fall
Upon the parched ground by heat updried;
No cooling moisture is perceived at all
Nor any show or sign of wet doth bide.

But as the fields, clothed with leaves and flowers,
The banks of roses smelling precious sweet,
Have but their beauty's date and timely hours,
And then, defaced by winter's cold and sleet,

So far as neither fruit nor form of flower
Stays for a witness what such branches bare,
But as time gave, time did again devour,
And changed our rising joy to falling care:

So of affection which our youth presented.
When she, that from the sun reaves power and light,
Did but decline her beams as discontented,
Converting sweetest days to saddest night,

All droops, all dies, all trodden under dust
The person, place, and passages forgotten;
The hardest steel eaten with softest rust,
The firm and solid tree both rent and rotten.

Those thoughts, so full of pleasure and content,
That in our absence were affection's food,
Are razed out and from the fancy rent,
In highest grace and heart's dear care that stood,

Are cast for prey to hatred and to scorn, –
Our dearest treasures and our heart's true joys;
The tokens hung on breast and kindly worn
Are now elsewhere disposed or held for toys.

And those which then our jealousy removed,
And others for our sakes then valued dear,
The one forgot, the rest are dear beloved,
When all of ours doth strange or vile appear.

Those streams seem standing puddles, which before
We saw our beauties in, so were they clear;
Belphoebe's course is now observed no more;

That fair resemblance weareth out of date.
Our ocean seas are but tempestuous waves,
And all things base, that blessed were of late . . .

And as a field, wherein the stubble stands
Of harvest past, the ploughman's eye offends;
He tills again, or tears them up with hands,
And throws to fire as foiled and fruitless ends,

And takes delight another seed to sow;
So doth the mind root up all wonted thought,
And scorns the care of our remaining woes:
The sorrows, which themselves for us have wrought,

Are burnt to cinders by new-kindled fires;
The ashes are dispersed into the air;
The sighs, the groans of all our past desires
Are clean outworn, as things that never were.

With youth is dead the hope of Love's return,
Who looks not back to hear our after-cries:
Where he is not, he laughs at those that mourn;
Whence he is gone, he scorns the mind that dies.

When he is absent, he believes no words;
When reason speaks, he, careless, stops his ears;
Whom he hath left, he never grace affords,
But bathes his wings in our lamenting tears.

Unlasting passion, soon outworn conceit,
Whereon I built, and on so dureless trust!
My mind had wounds. I dare not say deceit,
Were I resolved her promise was not just.

Sorrow was my revenge and woe my hate;
I powerless was to alter my desire;
My love is not of time or bound to date.
My heart's internal heat and living fire

Would not, or could, be quenched with sudden showers;
My bound respect was not confined to days;
My vowed faith not set to ended hours.
I love the bearing and not-bearing sprays

Which now to others do their sweetness send,
The incarnate, snow-driven white, and purest azure,
Who from high heaven doth on their fields descend,
Filling their barns with grain, and towers with treasure.

Erring or never erring, such is love
As, while it lasteth, scorns the account of those
Seeking but self-contentment to improve,
And hides, if any be, his inward woes,

And will not know, while he knows his own passion,
The often and unjust perseverance
In deeds of love and state, and every action
From that first day and year of their joy's entrance.

But I, unblessed and ill-born creature,
That did embrace the dust her body bearing,
That loved her, both by fancy and by nature,
That drew, even with the milk in my first sucking,

Affection from the parent's breast that bare me,
Have found her as a stranger so severe,
Improving my mishap in each degree;
But love was gone. So would I my life were!

A queen she was to me, no more Belphoebe;
A lion then, no more a milk-white dove;
A prisoner in her breast I could not be; –
She did untie the gentle chains of love.

Love was no more the love of hiding
All trespass and mischance for her own glory.
It had been such; it was still for the elect;
But I must be the example in love's story.
This was of all forepast the sad effect.

But thou, my weary soul and heavy thought,
Made by her love a burden to my being,
Dost know my error never was forethought,
Or ever could proceed from sense of loving.

Of other cause if then it had proceeding,
I leave the excuse, since judgment hath been given;
The limbs divided, sundered and ableeding,
Cannot complain the sentence was uneven.

This did that Nature's wonder, Virtue's choice,
The only paragon of Time's begetting,
Divine in words, angelical in voice,
That spring of joys, that flower of Love's own setting,

The idea remaining of those golden ages,
That beauty, braving heavens and earth embalming,
Which after worthless worlds but play on stages,
Such didst thou her long since describe, yet sighing

That thy unable spirit could not find aught,
In heaven's beauties or in earth's delight,
For likeness fit to satisfy thy thought:
But what hath it availed thee so to write?

She cares not for thy praise, who knows not theirs;
It's now an idle labour, and a tale
Told out of time, that dulls the hearer's ears,
A merchandise whereof there is no sale.

Leave them, or lay them up with thy despairs.
She hath resolved, and judged thee long ago.
Thy lines are now a murmuring to her ears,
Like to a falling stream, which, passing slow,

Is wont to nourish sleep and quietness;
So shall thy painful labours be perused,
And draw on rest, which sometime had regard;
But those her cares thy errors have excused.

Thy days fordone have had their day's reward;
So her hard heart, so her estranged mind,
In which above the heavens I once reposed,
So to thy error have her ears inclined,

And have forgotten all thy past deserving.
Holding in mind but only thine offence;
And only now affecteth thy depraving,
And thinks all vain that pleadeth thy defence.

Yet greater fancy beauty never bred;
A more desire the heart-blood never nourished;
Her sweetness an affection ever fed,
Which more in any age hath never flourished.

The mind and virtue never have begotten
A firmer love, since love on earth had power;
A love obscured, but cannot be forgotten;
Too great and strong for Time's jaws to devour,

Containing such a faith as ages wound not.
Care, wakeful ever of her good estate,
Fear, dreading loss, which sighs, and joys not
A memory of the joys her grace begat,

A lasting gratefulness for those comforts past
Of which the cordial sweetness cannot die –
These thoughts, knit up by faith, shall ever last;
These time assays, but never can untie,

Whose life once lived in her pearl-like breast,
Whose joys were drawn but from her happiness,
Whose heart's high pleasure and whose mind's true rest
Proceeded from her fortune's blessedness;

Who was intentive, wakeful, and dismayed
In fears, in dreams, in feverous jealousy,
Who long in silence served, and obeyed
With secret heart and hidden loyalty.

Which never change to sad adversity,
Which never age, or nature's overthrow,
Which never sickness or deformity,
Which never wasting care or wearing woe

(If subject unto these she could have been),
Which never words or wits malicious,
Which never honour's bait, or world's fame,
Achieved by attempts adventurous,
Or aught beneath the sun or heaven's frame

Can so dissolve, dissever, or destroy
The essential love of no frail parts compounded,
Though of the same now buried be the joy,
The hope, the comfort, and the sweetness ended,

But that the thoughts and memories of these
Work a relapse of passion, and remain
Of my sad heart the sorrow-sucking bees;
The wrongs received, the frowns persuade in vain.

And though these medicines work desire to end,
And are in others the true cure of liking,
The slaves that heal love's wounds, and do amend
Consuming woe, and slake our hearty sighing,

They work not so in thy mind's long decease.
External fancy time alone recureth,
All whose effects do wear away with ease.
Love of delight, while such delight endureth
Stays by the pleasure, but no longer stays.

But in my mind so is her love inclosed,
And is thereof not only the best part,
But into it the essence is disposed.
O love! (the more my woe) to it thou art

Even as the moisture in each plant that grows,
Even as the sun unto the frozen ground,
Even as the sweetness to the incarnate rose;
Even as the centre in each perfect round:

As water to the fish, to men as air,
As heat to fire, as light unto the sun.
Oh love! it is but vain to say *thou were*;
Ages and times cannot thy power outrun.

Thou art the soul of that unhappy mind
Which, being by nature made an idle thought,
Began even then to take immortal kind,
When first her virtues in thy spirits wrought.

From thee therefore that mover cannot move,
Because it is become thy cause of being;
Whatever error may obscure that love,
Whatever frail effect of mortal living,

Whatever passion from distempered heart,
What absence, time, or injuries effect,
What faithless friends or deep dissembled art
Present to feed her most unkind suspect.

Yet as the air in deep caves underground
Is strongly drawn when violent heat hath rent
Great clefts therein, till moisture do abound,
And then the same, imprisoned and up-pent,

Breaks out in earthquakes tearing all asunder;
So, in the centre of my cloven heart,
My heart, to whom her beauties were such wonder,
Lies the sharp poisoned head of that love's dart,

Which, till all break and all dissolve to dust,
Thence drawn it cannot be, or therein known.
There, mixed with my heart-blood, the fretting rust
The better part hath eaten and outgrown.

But what of those or these? or what of ought
Of that which was, or that which is, to treat?
What I possess is but the same I sought:
My love was false, my labours were deceit.

Nor less than such they are esteemed to be,
A fraud bought at the price of many woes,
A guile, whereof the profits unto me –
Could it be thought premeditate for those?

Witness those withered leaves left on the tree,
The sorrow-worn face, the pensive mind;
The external shews what may the internal be.
Cold care hath bitten both the root and rind.

But stay, my thoughts, make end: give fortune way.
Harsh is the voice of woe and sorrow's sound.
Complaints cure not, and tears do but allay
Griefs for a time, which after more abound.

To seek for moisture in the Arabian sand
Is but a loss of labour and of rest.
The links which time did break of hearty bands

Words cannot knit, or wailings make anew.
Seek not the sun in clouds when it is set.
On highest mountains, where those cedars grew,
Against whose banks the troubled ocean bet,

And were the marks to find thy hoped port,
Into a soil far off themselves remove.
On Sestus' shore, Leander's late resort,
Hero hath left no lamp to guide her love;

Thou lookest for light in vain, and storms arise;
She sleeps thy death, that erst thy danger sighed.
Strive then no more, bow down thy weary eyes,
Eyes which to all these woes thy heart have guided.

She is gone, she is lost! she is found, she is ever fair!
Sorrow draws weakly, where love draws not too:
Woe's cries sound nothing, but only in love's ear.
Do then by dying what life cannot do.

Unfold thy flocks and leave them to the fields
To feed on hills, or dales, where likes them best,
Of what the summer or the spring-time yields,
For love and time hath given thee leave to rest.

Thy heart which was their fold, now in decay
By often storms and winter's many blasts,
All torn and rent becomes misfortune's prey;
False hope my shepherd's staff, now age hath brast.

My pipe, which love's own hand gave my desire
To sing her praises and my woe upon,
Despair hath often threatened to the fire,
As vain to keep now all the rest are gone.


Thus home I draw, as death's long night draws on;
Yet every foot, old thoughts turn back mine eyes:
Constraint me guides, as old age draws a stone
Against the hill, which over-weighty lies

For feeble arms or wasted strength to move.
My steps are backward, gazing on my loss,
My mind's affection and my soul's sole love,
Not mixed with fancy's chaff or fortune's dross.

To God I leave it, who first gave it me,
And I her gave, and she returned again,
As it was hers. So let His mercies be
Of my last comforts the essential mean.
       But be it so or not, the effects are past.
       Her love hath end; my woe must ever last.

## 9 The End of the Books of the Ocean's Love to Cynthia, and the Beginning of the Two-and-Twentieth Book, Entreating of Sorrow

My days' delights, my spring-time joys fordone,
Which in the dawn and rising sun of youth
Had their creation, and were first begun,

Do in the evening and the winter sad
Present my mind, which takes my time's account,
The grief remaining of the joy it had.

My times that then ran over themselves in these,
And now run out in other's happiness,
Bring unto those new joys and new-born days.

So could she not if she were not the sun,
Which sees the birth, and burial, of all else,
And holds that power with which she first begun,

Leaving each withered body to be torn
By fortune, and by times tempestuous,
Which, by her virtue, once fair fruit have borne,

Knowing she can renew, and can create
Green from the ground, and flowers even out of stone,
By virtue lasting over time and date,

Leaving us only woe, which, like the moss,
Having compassion of unburied bones,
Cleaves to mischance, and unrepaired loss.

For tender stalks . . .

## 10 A Vision upon this Conceit of *The Faerie Queene*

Methought I saw the grave where Laura lay
Within that temple where the vestal flame
Was wont to burn: and, passing by that way,
To see that buried dust of living fame,
Whose tomb fair Love and fairer Virtue kept,
All suddenly I saw the Fairy Queen,
At whose approach the soul of Petrarch wept;
And from thenceforth those graces were not seen.
For they this Queen attended; in whose stead
Oblivion laid him down on Laura's hearse.
Hereat the hardest stones were seen to bleed,
And groans of buried ghosts the heavens did pierce:
　　Where Homer's sprite did tremble all for grief,
　　　And cursed the access of that celestial thief.

## 11 Another of the Same

The praise of meaner wits this work like profit brings
As doth the cuckoo's song delight when Philomena sings.
If thou hast formed right true virtue's face herein,
Virtue herself can best discern, to whom they written been.
If thou hast beauty praised, let her sole looks divine
Judge if aught therein be amiss, and mend it by her eyne.
If Chastity want aught, or Temperance her due,
Behold her princely mind aright, and write thy Queen anew.
Meanwhile she shall perceive how far her virtues soar
Above the reach of all that live, or such as wrote of yore:
And thereby will excuse and favour thy good will,
Whose virtue cannot be expressed but by an angel's quill.
    Of me no lines are loved nor letters are of price,
    Of all which speak our English tongue, but those of thy
      device.

## 12 Farewell to the Court

Like truthless dreams, so are my joys expired,
And past return are all my dandled days,
My love misled, and fancy quite retired;
Of all which past, the sorrow only stays.

My lost delights, now clean from sight of land,
Have left me all alone in unknown ways,
My mind to woe, my life in fortune's hand;
Of all which past, the sorrow only stays.

As in a country strange without companion,
I only wail the wrong of death's delays,
Whose sweet spring spent, whose summer well nigh done;
Of all which past, the sorrow only stays;

Whom care forewarns, ere age and winter cold,
To haste me hence to find my fortune's fold.

## 13 Now We Have Present Made

Now we have present made
To Cynthia, Phoebe, Flora,
Diana and Aurora,
Beauty that cannot fade,

A flower of Love's own planting,
A pattern kept by Nature
For beauty, form and stature
When she would frame a darling.

She is the valley of Peru
Whose summer ever lasteth.
Time conquering all she mastereth
By being always new.

As elemental fire
Whose food and flame consumes not,
Or as the passion ends not
Of virtue's true desire,

So her celestial frame
And quintessential mind,
Which heavens together bind,
Shall ever be the same.

Then to her servants leave her,
Love, Nature and Affection,
Princess of world's perfection.
Our praises but deceive her.

If Love could find a quill
Drawn from an angel's wing,
Or did the Muses sing
That pretty wanton's will,

Perchance he could indict
To please all other sense;
But love's and woe's expense
Sorrow can only write.

## 14  If Cynthia be a Queen, a Princess and Supreme

If Cynthia be a queen, a princess and supreme,
Keep these among the rest, or say it was a dream;
For those that like, expound, and those that loathe, express
Meanings according as their minds are moved more or less.
For writing what thou art, or showing what thou were,
Adds to the one disdain, to the other but despair.
Thy mind of neither needs, in both seeing it exceeds.

## 15 My Body in the Walls Captived

My body in the walls captived
Feels not the wounds of spiteful envy;
But my thralled mind, of liberty deprived,
Fast fettered in her ancient memory,
Doth nought behold but sorrow's dying face.
Such prison erst was so delightful,
As it desired no other dwelling place:
But time's effects and destinies despiteful
Have changed both my keeper and my fare.
Love's fire and beauty's light I then had store;
But now, close kept, as captives wonted are,
That food, that heat, that light, I find no more.
    Despair bolts up my doors; and I alone
    Speak to dead walls; but those hear not my moan.

## 16  To the Translator of Lucan

Had Lucan hid the truth to please the time
He had been too unworthy of thy pen,
Who never sought nor ever cared to climb
By flattery, or seeking worthless men.
For this thou hast been bruised; but yet those scars
Do beautify no less than those wounds do
Received in just and in religious wars;
Though thou hast bled by both, and bearest them too.
Change not! To change thy fortune 'tis too late.
Who with a manly faith resolves to die,
May promise to himself a lasting state,
Though not so great, yet free from infamy.
   Such was thy Lucan, whom so to translate,
   Nature thy muse like Lucan's did create.

## 17 A Petition to Queen Anne

My day's delight, my spring-time joys fordone,
Which in the dawn and rising sun of youth
Had their creation and were first begun,

Do in the evening and the winter sad
Present my mind, which takes my time's account,
The griefs remaining of the joy it had.

My tender stalks, now clad with rugged rinds,
Whose former fruit was of such mixture made
As with the harmful blast and eastern wind

In crept the eating worm, and in the heart
And kernel taketh nourishment
Till it had all devoured the better part;

Which when my wants presented to my taste,
Then hopeful of the good mine own hands planted
Of all my toil I found false fruit at last,

Love all eaten out but in outward show,
My elder fortune cut by new mishap,
The false internal then I only knew.

For as no fortune stands, so no man's love
Stays by the wretched and disconsolate;
All old affections from new sorrows move.

Moss by unburied bones, ivy by walls,
Whom life and people have abandoned,
Till the one be rotten stays, till the other falls;

But friendships, kindred and love's memory
Die, cool, extinguish, hearing or beholding
The voice of woe or face of misery.

For friends in all are like those winter showers
Which come uncalled, but then forebear to fall
When harmful heat hath burnt both leaves and flowers.

Then what we sometime were they know no more
Whenas those storms of powerful destiny
Have once defaced the form we had before.

For if there did in cinders but remain
The smallest heat of love's long-lasting fires
I could not call for right and call in vain,

Or, had truth power, the guiltless could not fall,
Malice win glory or revenge triumph.
But truth alone cannot encounter all.

All love, and all desert of former times
Malice hath covered from my sovereign's eyes
And largely abroad suspected crimes,

Burying the former with their memory,
Teaching Offence to speak before it go,
Disguising private hate with public duty.

Cold walls, to you I sigh, but you are senseless,
Yet senseful all alike as are those friends,
Friends only of my sometime happiness.

To whom then shall I cry? to whom shall wrong
Cast down her tears or hold up folded hands?
To her to whom compassion doth belong.

To her who is the first, and may alone
Be called Empress of the Brittannies.
Who should have mercy if a queen have none?

Who can resist strong hate, fierce injury?
Or who relieve the oppressed state of truth
Who is companion else to powerful majesty?

But you, great, goodliest, graceful princess,
Who hath brought glory and prosperity
Unto a widow's land and people hopeless,

Perfect our comfort by protecting those
Whom hate and no self-guile hath ruined.
All in the field are yours, whatever grows,

As well the humble briar under shade
As are the tallest cedars which obscure them.
Love, Nature, Right have you their princess made;

Save then your own, whose life in your defence
I scorned to keep and could have joyed to lose;
For love, destruction is no recompense.

If I have sold my duty, sold my faith
To strangers, which was only due to one,
Nothing I should esteem as dear as death,

But if both God and time shall make you know
That I, your humble vassal, am oppressed,
Then cast your eyes on undeserved woe,

That I and mine may never mourn the miss
Of her we had, but praise our living Queen
Who brings us equal, if no greater, bliss.

## 18 A Farewell to False Love

[Answered by No. 62]

Farewell, false Love, thou oracle of lies,
A mortal foe, an enemy to rest,
An envious boy from whom all cares arise,
A bastard born, a beast with rage possessed,
A way of error, a temple full of treason,
In all effects contrary unto reason;

A poisoned serpent, covered all with flowers,
Mother of sighs and murderer of repose,
A sea of sorrows, from whence are drawn such showers
As moisture lends to every grief that grows;
A school of guile, a nest of deep deceit,
A gilded hook that holds a poisoned bait;

A fortress foiled whom reason did defend,
A siren song, a fever of the mind,
A maze wherein affection finds no end,
A ranging cloud that runs before the wind,
A substance like the shadow of the sun,
A goal of grief for which the wisest run.

## 19 An Epitaph Upon the Right Honourable Sir Philip Sidney, Knight

To praise thy life or wail thy worthy death
And want thy wit, thy wit high, pure, divine,
Is far beyond the power of mortal line,
Nor any one hath worth that draweth breath;

Yet rich in zeal, though poor in learning's lore,
And friendly care, obscured in secret breast,
And love, that envy in thy life suppressed,
Thy dear life done, thy death hath doubled more,

And I, that in thy time and living state
Did only praise thy virtues in my thought,
As one that seld the rising sun hath sought,
With words and tears now wail thy timeless fate.

Drawn was thy race aright from princely line;
Nor less than such, by gifts that nature gave,
The common mother that all creatures have,
Doth virtue show, and princely lineage shine.

A king gave thee thy name; a kingly mind,
That God thee gave, who found it now too dear
For this base world, and hath resumed it near
To sit in skies, and sort with powers divine.

Kent thy birth-days, and Oxford held thy youth;
The heavens made haste, and stayed nor years nor time;
The fruits of age grew ripe in thy first prime;
Thy will, thy words; thy words the seals of truth.

Great gifts and wisdom rare employed thee thence,
To treat from kings with those more great than kings;
Such hope men had to lay the highest things
On thy wise youth, to be transported hence.

Whence to sharp wars sweet honour did thee call,
Thy country's love, religion, and thy friends
(Of worthy men the marks, the lives, and ends)
And her defence, for whom we labour all.

There didst thou vanquish shame and tedious age,
Grief, sorrow, sickness, and base fortune's might;
Thy rising day saw never woeful night,
But passed with praise from off this worldly stage.

Back to the camp by thee that day was brought,
First, thine own death, and after, thy long fame;
Tears to the soldiers; the proud Castilians shame;
Virtue expressed, and honour truly taught.

What hath he lost that such great grace hath won?
Young years for endless years, and hope unsure
Of fortune's gifts for wealth that still shall dure:
O happy race, with so great praises run!

England doth hold thy limbs, that bred the same;
Flanders thy valour, where it last was tried;
The camp thy sorrow, where thy body died;
Thy friends thy want; the world thy virtue's fame;

Nations thy wit. Our minds lay up thy love;
Letters thy learning; thy loss long years to come.
In worthy hearts sorrow hath made thy tomb;
Thy soul and sprite enrich the heavens above.

The liberal heart embalmed in grateful tears,
Young sighs, sweet sighs, sage sighs, bewail thy fall;
Envy her sting, and spite hath left her gall;
Malice herself a mourning garment wears.

That day their Hannibal died, our Scipio fell, –
Scipio, Cicero, and Petrarch of our time;
Whose virtues, wounded by my worthless rhyme,
Let angels speak, and heaven thy praises tell.

## 20 Fortune Hath Taken Thee Away, My Love

[Answered by No. 44]

Fortune hath taken thee away, my love,
My life's joy and my soul's heaven above;
Fortune hath taken thee away, my princess,
My world's delight and my true fancy's mistress.

Fortune hath taken all away from me,
Fortune hath taken all by taking thee;
Dead to all joys, I only live to woe,
So Fortune now becomes my fancy's foe.

In vain, mine eyes, in vain you waste your tears;
In vain, my sighs, the smokes of my despairs,
In vain you search the earth and heavens above,
In vain you search, for Fortune keeps my love.

Then will I leave my love in Fortune's hands,
Then will I leave my love in worthless bands,
And only love the sorrow due to me,
Sorrow henceforth that shall my princess be,

And only joy that Fortune conquers kings.
Fortune that rules on earth and earthly things
Hath taken my love in spite of virtue's might.
So blind a goddess did never virtue right.

With Wisdom's eyes had but blind Fortune seen,
Then had my love my love for ever been;
But Love, farewell; though Fortune conquer thee,
No fortune base shall ever alter me.

Calling to mind mine eye went long about
To cause my heart for to forsake my breast,
All in a rage I thought to pull it out,
By whose device I lived in such unrest.
What could it say then to regain my grace? –
Forsooth, that it had seen my mistress' face.

Another time, I called unto mind,
It was my heart which all this woe had wrought,
Because that he to Love his fort resigned,
When on such wars my fancy never thought.
What could he say when I would him have slain? –
That he was yours, and had forgone me clean.

At length, when I perceived both eye and heart
Excuse themselves, as guiltless of mine ill,
I found myself the cause of all my smart,
And told myself, 'Myself now slay I will.'
Yet when I saw myself to you was true,
I loved myself, because myself loved you.

## 22 The Nymph's Reply to the Shepherd*

[An answer to No. 42]

If all the world and love were young
And truth in every shepherd's tongue,
These pretty pleasures might me move
To live with thee and be thy love.

Time drives the flocks from field to fold,
When rivers rage and rocks grow cold,
And Philomel becometh dumb;
The rest complains of cares to come.

The flowers do fade, and wanton fields
To wayward winter reckoning yields:
A honey tongue, a heart of gall,
Is fancy's spring, but sorrow's fall.

Thy gowns, thy shoes, thy beds of roses,
Thy cap, thy kirtle, and thy posies,
Soon break, soon wither, soon forgotten,
In folly ripe, in reason rotten.

Thy belt of straw and ivy buds,
Thy coral clasps and amber studs,
All these in me no means can move
To come to thee and be thy love.

But could youth last, and love still breed,
Had joys no date, nor age no need,
Then those delights my mind might move
To live with thee and be thy love.

## 23  A Secret Murder Hath Been Done of Late*

A secret murder hath been done of late,
Unkindness found to be the bloody knife,
And she that did the deed a dame of state,
Fair, gracious, wise as any beareth life.

To quit herself this answer did she make:
'Mistrust,' quoth she, 'hath brought him to this end,
Which makes the man so much himself mistake
To lay the guilt unto his guiltless friend.'

Lady, not so; not feared I found my death,
For no desert thus murdered is my mind;
And yet before I yield my fainting breath
I quit the killer though I blame the kind.

> You kill, unkind; I die, and yet am true.
> For at your sight my wound doth bleed anew.

## 24 Sought by the World, and Hath the World Disdained*

Sought by the world, and hath the world disdained,
Is she, my heart, for whom thou dost endure,
Unto whose grace, since Kings have not obtained,
Sweet is thy choice though loss of life be sour;
    Yet to the man whose youth such pains must prove
    No better end than that which comes by love.

Steer then thy course unto the port of death,
Since thy hard hap no better hap may find,
Where when thou shalt unlade thy latest breath
Envy herself shall swim to save thy mind
    Whose body sunk in search to gain that shore
    Where many a prince had perished before.

And yet, my heart, it might have been foreseen,
Since skilful medicines mends each kind of grief,
Then in my breast full safely hadst thou been;
But thou, my heart, wouldst never me believe,
    Who told thee true when first thou didst aspire
    Death was the end of every such desire.

## 25  What Else is Hell but Loss of Blissful Heaven?*

What else is hell but loss of blissful heaven?
What darkness but lacks of lightsome day?
What else is death but things of life beriven?
What winter else but pleasant spring's decay?

Unrest what else but fancy's hot desire,
Fed with delay and followed with despair?
What else mishap but longing to aspire,
To strive against earth, water, fire and air?

Heaven were my state and happy sunshine day,
And life most blest, to joy one hour's desire;
Hap, bliss and rest and sweet springtime of May
Were to behold my fair consuming fire.

But lo, I feel, by absence from your sight,
Mishap, unrest, death, winter, hell, dark night.

## 26 On the Cards and the Dice*

Before the sixth day of the next new year
Strange wonders in this kingdom shall appear:
Four kings shall be assembled in this isle,
Where they shall keep great tumult for a while.
Many men then shall have an end of crosses,
And many likewise shall sustain great losses;
Many that now full joyful are and glad
Shall at that time be sorrowful and sad.
Full many a Christian's heart shall quake for fear,
The dreadful sound of trump when he shall hear.
Dead bones shall then be tumbled up and down,
In every city and in every town.
By day or night this tumult shall not cease,
Until an herald shall proclaim a peace,
An herald strange, the like was never born,
Whose very beard is flesh and mouth is horn.

## 27 Sweet Are the Thoughts where Hope Persuadeth Hap*

Sweet are the thoughts where Hope persuadeth Hap,
Great are the joys where Heart obtains request,
Dainty the life nursed still in Fortune's lap,
Much is the ease where troubled minds find rest.
These are the fruits that valour doth advance
And cuts off dread by hope of happy chance.

Thus hope brings hap but to the worthy wight,
Thus pleasure comes but after hard assay,
Thus fortune yields in mauger of her spite,
Thus happy state is won without delay.
Then must I needs advance myself by skill,
And live to serve in hope of your good will.

## 28  A Poesy to Prove Affection Is not Love*

Conceit begotten by the eyes
Is quickly born and quickly dies;
For while it seeks our hearts to have,
Meanwhile, there reason makes his grave;
For many things the eyes approve,
Which yet the heart doth seldom love.

For as the seeds in spring time sown
Die in the ground ere they be grown,
Such is conceit, whose rooting fails,
As child that in the cradle quails
Or else within the mother's womb
Hath his beginning and his tomb.

Affection follows Fortune's wheels,
And soon is shaken from her heels,
For, following beauty or estate,
Her liking still is turned to hate.
For all affections have their change,
And fancy only loves to range.

Desire himself runs out of breath,
And, getting, doth but gain his death:
Desire nor reason hath nor rest,
And, blind, doth seldom choose the best.
Desire attained is not desire,
But as the cinders of the fire.

As ships in ports desired are drowned,
As fruit, once ripe, then falls to ground,
As flies that seek for flames are brought
To cinders by the flames they sought;
So fond desire when it attains,
The life expires, the woe remains.

And yet some poets fain would prove
Affection to be perfect love,
And that desire is of that kind,
No less a passion of the mind,
As if wild beasts and men did seek
To like, to love, to choose alike.

## 29  A Poem Put into My Lady Leighton's Pocket*

Lady, farewell, whom I in silence serve;
    Would God thou knewest the depth of my desire.
Then might I hope, though nought I can deserve,
    Some drop of grace would quench my scorching fire.
But as to love unknown I have decreed,
So spare to speak doth often spare to speed.

Yet better 'twere that I in woe should waste
    Than sue for grace and pity in despite,
And though I see in thee such pleasure placed
    That feeds my joy and breeds my chief delight,
Withall I see a chaste content disdain
Their suits which seek to win thy will again.

Then farewell hope and help to each man's harm,
    The wind of woe hath torn my tree of trust.
Care quench'd the coals which did my fancy warm
    And all my help lies buried in the dust.
But yet amongst those cares which cross my rest
This comfort grows; I think I love thee best.

## 30 Feed Still Thyself, Thou Fondling, with Belief*

Feed still thyself, thou fondling, with belief,
Go hunt thy hope that never took effect,
Accuse the wrongs that oft hath wrought thy grief
And reckon sure where reason would suspect.

Dwell in the dreams of wish and vain desire.
Pursue the faith that flies and seeks to new,
Run after hopes that mock thee with retire
And look for love where liking never grew.

Devise conceits to ease thy careful heart,
Trust upon times and days of grace behind,
Presume the rights of promise and desert
And measure love by thy believing mind.

Force thy affects that spite doth daily chase.
Wink at thy wrongs with wilful oversight,
See not the soil and stain of thy disgrace,
Nor reck disdain, to dote on thy delight.

And when thou seest the end of thy reward,
And these effects ensue of thine assault,
When rashness rues that reason should regard,
Yet still accuse thy fortune for the fault

> And cry, O love, O death, O vain desire,
> When thou complainest the heat and feeds the fire.

## 31  Like to a Hermit Poor in Place Obscure*

Like to a hermit poor in place obscure
I mean to spend my days of endless doubt,
To wail such woes as time cannot recure,
Where nought but Love shall ever find me out.

My food shall be of care and sorrow made;
My drink nought else but tears fallen from mine eyes;
And for my light, in such obscured shade,
The flames shall serve which from my heart arise.

A gown of grief my body shall attire,
My staff of broken hope whereon I'll stay;
Of late repentance linked with long desire
The couch is framed whereon my limbs I'll lay.

    And at my gates Despair shall linger still,
    To let in Death when Love and Fortune will.

## 32 My First-Born Love, Unhappily Conceived*

My first-born love, unhappily conceived,
Brought forth in pain and christened with a curse,
Die in your infancy, of life bereaved
    By your cruel nurse.

Restless desire that from my love proceeded,
Leave to be, and seek your heaven by dying,
Since you, O you, your own hope have exceeded
    By too high flying.

And you, my words, my heart's faithful expounders,
No more offer your jewel unesteemed,
Since those eyes, my love's life and lives' confounders,
    Your worth misdeemed.

Love, leave to desire, words, leave it to utter,
Swell on, my thoughts, till you break that contains you;
My complaints in those deaf ears no more mutter
    That so disdains you.

And you, careless of me, without feeling,
With dry eyes behold my tragedy smiling;
Deck your proud triumphs with your poor slave's yielding
    To his own spoiling.

But if that wrong or holy truth despised
To just revenge the heavens ever moved,
So let her love and be still denied,
    Who she so loved.

## 33 The Advice*

Many desire, but few or none deserve
To win the fort of thy most constant will;
Therefore take heed; let fancy never swerve
But unto him that will defend thee still.
        For this be sure, the fort of fame once won,
        Farewell the rest, thy happy days are done.

Many desire, but few or none deserve
To pluck the flowers and let the leaves to fall;
Therefore take heed; let fancy never swerve
But unto him that will take leaves and all.
        For this be sure, the flower once plucked away,
        Farewell the rest, thy happy days decay.

Many desire, but few or none deserve
To cut the corn not subject to the sickle;
Therefore take heed; let fancy never swerve,
But constant stand, for mowers' minds are fickle;
        For this be sure, the crop being once obtained,
        Farewell the rest, the soil will be disdained.

## 34 Sir Walter Ralegh to His Son*

Three things there be that prosper all apace
And flourish while they are asunder far,
But on a day, they meet all in a place,
And when they meet, they one another mar.

And they be these; the Wood, the Weed, the Wag:
The Wood is that that makes the gallows tree;
The Weed is that that strings the hangman's bag;
The Wag, my pretty knave, betokens thee.

Now mark, dear boy, while these assemble not,
Green springs the tree, hemp grows, the wag is wild;
But when they meet, it makes the timber rot,
It frets the halter, and it chokes the child.

## 35  An Epigram on Henry Noel

['Noe–L'; answered by No. 60]

The word of denial and the letter of fifty
Makes the gentleman's name that will never be thrifty.

## 36  Sir W. Ralegh on the Snuff of a Candle the Night before He Died*

Cowards fear to die, but courage stout,
Rather than live in snuff, will be put out.

## 37  De Morte*

Man's life's a tragedy: his mother's womb,
From which he enters, is the tiring room;
This spacious earth the theatre; and the stage
That country which he lives in: passions, rage,
Folly, and vice are actors; the first cry,
The prologue to the ensuing tragedy;
The former act consisteth of dumb shows;
The second, he to more perfection grows;
In the third he is a man, and doth begin
To nurture vice, and act the deeds of sin;
In the fourth, declines; in the fifth, diseases clog
And trouble him; then death's his epilogue.

Sweet were the sauce would please each kind of taste;
The life likewise were pure that never swerved:
For spiteful tongues in cankered stomachs placed
Deem worst of things which best (percase) deserved.
But what for that? This medicine may suffice
To scorn the rest, and seek to please the wise.

Though sundry minds in sundry sort do deem,
Yet worthiest wights yield praise for every pain;
But envious brains do nought, or light, esteem
Such stately steps as they cannot attain.
For whoso reaps renown above the rest,
With heaps of hate shall surely be oppressed.

Wherefore, to write my censure of this book,
This Glass of Steel unpartially doth show
Abuses all to such as in it look,
From prince to poor, from high estate to low.
As for the verse, who list like trade to try,
I fear me much, shall hardly reach so high.

## 39 Verse Translations from the *History of the World*

1 BOOK 1, CHAPTER 1.6: Virgil, *Aeneid* 6.724–7

The heaven and earth and all the liquid main,
The moon's bright globe and stars Titanian
A spirit within maintains; and their whole mass
A mind, which through each part infused doth pass,
Fashions and works, and wholly doth transpierce
All this great body of the universe.

2 BOOK 1, CHAPTER 1.7: Ovid, *Metamorphoses*
4.226–8

The world discerns itself, while I the world behold;
By me the longest years and other times are told;
I, the world's eye.

3 BOOK 1, CHAPTER 1.11: Ovid, *Tristia* and Juvenal,
*Satires* 7.201

'Gainst fate no counsel can prevail.
Kingdoms to slaves by destiny,
To captives triumphs given be.

4 BOOK 1, CHAPTER 1.15: Athenaeus (cf. Aristotle,
*Nichomachean Ethics*, 6.4)

From wisdom fortune differs far;
And yet in works most like they are.

5 BOOK 1, CHAPTER 1.15: Ovid, *Remedia Amoris*
(*Cure for Love*) 119

While fury gallops on the way
Let no man's fury's gallop stay.

6  BOOK 1, CHAPTER 2.1: Ovid, *Metamorphoses* 1.76–8

More holy than the rest, and understanding more,
A living creature wants, to rule all made before;
So man began to be.


7  BOOK 1, CHAPTER 2.3: Claudius Marius Victor
(*de perversis suae aet. moribus*) Epist. 30–1

Diseases, famine, enemies, in us no change have wrought;
What erst we were, we are; still in the same snare caught:
   No time can our corrupted manners mend;
   In vice we dwell, in sin that hath no end.


8  BOOK 1, CHAPTER 2.5: Ovid, *Metamorphoses* 1.414–15

From thence our kind hard-hearted is, enduring pain
   and care;
Approving that our bodies of a stony nature are.


9  BOOK 1, CHAPTER 2.5: Albinovanus, *Elegy on the
Death of Maecenas*, 113–14

The plants and trees made poor and old
   By winter envious,
   The spring-time bounteous
Covers again from shame and cold;
But never man repaired again
      His youth and beauty lost,
      Though art and care and cost
Do promise nature's help in vain.


10  BOOK 1, CHAPTER 2.5: Catullus, *Poems* 5.4–5

The sun may set and rise;
But we, contrariwise,
Sleep after our short light
One everlasting night.

11 BOOK 1, CHAPTER 3.3: Ovid, *Metamorphoses* 1.61–2

The East wind with Aurora hath abiding
  Among the Arabian and the Persian hills,
Whom Phoebus first salutes at his uprising.


12 BOOK 1, CHAPTER 3.3: Ovid, *Metamorphoses*
1.107–8

The joyful spring did ever last, and Zephyrus did breed
Sweet flowers by his gentle blast, without the help
  of seed.


13 BOOK 1, CHAPTER 4.2: Virgil, *Aeneid* 1.490–1

The Amazon with crescent-formed shield
Penthesilea leads into the field.


14 BOOK 1, CHAPTER 5.5: Lucan, *Pharsalia* 4.373–8, 380–1

O wasteful riot, never well content
  With low-priced fare; hunger ambitious
Of cates by land and sea far fetched and sent;
  Vain glory of a table sumptuous;
Learn with how little life may be preserved.
  In gold and myrrh they need not to carouse;
But with the brook the people's thirst is served,
Who, fed with bread and water, are not starved.


15 BOOK 1, CHAPTER 7.3: Anaxandr. Rhod. ap.
Natal. Com. 1.7; p. 12, ed. 1612

I sacrifice to God the beef which you adore;
I broil the Egyptian eels, which you as God implore;
You fear to eat the flesh of swine; I find it sweet;
You worship dogs; to bear them I think meet,
When they my store devour.

The Egyptians think it sin to root up or to bite
Their leeks or onions, which they serve with holy rite.
    O happy nations, which of their own sowing
    Have store of gods in every garden growing!

17  BOOK 1, CHAPTER 6.5: Callimachus, *Hymn to Zeus* 8–9

The Cretans ever liars were; they care not what they say;
For they a tomb have built for thee, O king that livest alway.

18  BOOK 1, CHAPTER 6.7: Euripides, fragment *Melanippus*
6 (Dindorf)

Heaven and earth did one form bear;
But when disjoined once they were
    From mutual embraces,
All things to light appeared then;
Of trees, birds, beasts, fishes and men
    The still remaining races.

19  BOOK 1, CHAPTER 6.7: Orpheus to Musaeus, fragment 1
from Just. Mart., *Cohort ad Gent.* 15

Then marking this my sacred speech, but truly lend
Thy heart that's reason's sphere, and the right way ascend,
And see the world's sole king. First, He is simply one
Begotten of Himself, from whom is born alone
All else, in which He's still; nor could it ever befall
A mortal eye to see Him once, yet he sees all.

20  BOOK 1, CHAPTER 6.7: Orpheus to Musaeus,
fragment 6 from Proclus

The first of all is God, and the same last is He.
God is the head and midst; yea, from Him all things be.
God is the base of earth and of the starred sky;

He is the male and female too; never shall die.
The spirit of all is God; the sun and moon and what is higher;
The king, the original of all, of all the end:
For close in holy breast He all did comprehend;
Whence all to blessed His wondrous power did send.

21 BOOK 1, CHAPTER 7.3: Virgil, *Aeneid* 8.318–23

Saturn descending from the heavens high,
     Fearing the arms of Jupiter his son,
His kingdom lost, and banished, thence did fly.
     Rude people on the mountain tops he won
To live together, and by laws; which done,
     He chose to call it Latium.

22 BOOK 1, CHAPTER 7.7: Ovid, *Fasti* (*Festival Calendar*)
1.103–4

The ancients called me Chaos; my great years
By those old times of which I sing appears.

23 BOOK 1, CHAPTER 8.3: Lucan, *Pharsalia* 4.131–5

The moistened osier of the hoary willow
     Is woven first into a little boat;
Then, clothed in bullock's hide, upon the billow
     Of a proud river lightly doth it float
          Under the waterman:
     So on the lakes of overswelling Po
     Sails the Venetian; and the Briton so
          On the outspread ocean.

24 BOOK 1, CHAPTER 8.4: Apollonius of Rhodes,
*Argonautica* (*Voyage of the Argonauts*) 2.1004–6

The Chalybes plough not their barren soil,
     But undermine high hills for iron veins;

Changing the purchase of their endless toil
  For merchandise, which their poor lives sustains.


25  BOOK 1, CHAPTER 8.2: NOTE 2: Ovid *Fasti*
(*Festival Calendar*) 2.289–90

The Arcadians the earth inhabited
Ere yet the moon did shine, or Jove was bred.


26  BOOK 1, CHAPTER 10.7: Sedulius 1.226–31

Ah! wretched they that worship vanities,
  And consecrate dumb idols in their heart;
Who their own maker, God on high, despise,
  And fear the work of their own hands and art!

What fury, what great madness, doth beguile
  Men's minds, that man should ugly shapes
  adore,
Of birds or bulls or dragons, or the vile
  Half-dog, half-man, on knees for aid implore!


27  BOOK 1, CHAPTER 11.8: Lucretius, *On the Nature of
Things* 2.54–5

We fear by light, as children in the dark.


28  BOOK 2, CHAPTER 6.4: Aeschylus, *Prometheus
Bound*, 456–61

But fortune governed all their works, till when
  I first found out how stars did set and rise, –
A profitable art to mortal men.
  And others of like use I did devise:
  As letters to compose in learned wise
I first did teach, and first did amplify
The mother of the Muses, Memory.

29  BOOK 2, CHAPTER 7.3, NOTE 3: Sidonius, *Songs* 17.15–16

I have no wine of Gaza nor Falerna wine
Nor any for thy drinking of Sarepta's vine.

30  BOOK 2, CHAPTER 7.4, NOTE 5: Virgil, *Aeneid* 1.728–30

The queen anon commands the weighty bowl,
Weighty with precious stones and massy gold,
To flow with wine. This Belus used of old,
    And all of Belus' line.

31  BOOK 2, CHAPTER 8.1: Lucan, *Pharsalia* 3.220–1

Phoenicians first, if fame may credit have,
In rude characters dared our words to grave.

32  BOOK 2, CHAPTER 8.1: Diogenes Laertius 7.30

If a Phoenician born I am, what then?
    Cadmus was so; to whom Greece owes
The books of learned men.

33  BOOK 2, CHAPTER 10.2: Tibullus, 1.7.18

The white dove is for holy held in Syria Palestine.

34  BOOK 2, CHAPTER 13.3: Ovid, *Amores* 2.43–4

Here Tantalus in water seeks for water, and doth miss
The fleeting fruit he catcheth at; his long tongue brought him
    this.

35  BOOK 2, CHAPTER 13.3: Horace, *Satires*, 1, 1. 68–70

The thirsting Tantalus doth catch at streams that from him
    flee;
Why laughest thou? The name but changed, the tale is told
    of thee.

Strong Ilion thou shalt see with walls and towers high,
Built with the harp of wise Apollo's harmony.

The brazen tower, with doors close barred,
And watchful bandogs' frightful guard,
    Kept safe the maidenhead
Of Danae from secret love,
Till smiling Venus and wise Jove
    Beguiled her father's dread:
For, changed into a golden shower,
The god into her lap did pour
    Himself and took his pleasure.
Though guards and stony walls to break
The thunderbolt is far more weak
    Than is a golden treasure.

If all this world had no original,
    But things have ever been as now they are
Before the siege of Thebes or Troy's last fall,
    Why did no poet sing some elder war?

In the main sea the isle of Crete doth lie,
Whence Jove was born; thence is our progeny.
There is Mount Ida; there in fruitful land
An hundred great and godly cities stand.
Thence, if I follow not mistaken fame,
Teucer, the eldest of our grandsires came
To the Rhoetean shores, and reigned there

Ere yet fair Ilion was built, and ere
The towers of Troy. Their dwelling-place they sought
In lowest vales. Hence Cybel's rites were brought;
Hence Corybantian cymbals did remove;
And hence the name of our Idaean grove.


40   BOOK 2, CHAPTER 14.1: Virgil, *Aeneid* 3.163–8

Hesperia the Grecians call the place –
An ancient fruitful land, a warlike race.
Oenotrians held it; now the later progeny
Gives it their captain's name and calls it Italy.
This seat belongs to us; hence Dardanus,
Hence came the author of our stock, Iasius.


41   BOOK 2, CHAPTER 14.1: Virgil, *Aeneid* 7.205–11

Some old Auruncans, I remember well –
Though time have made the fame obscure – would tell
Of Dardanus, how born in Italy;
From hence he into Phrygia did fly.
And leaving Tuscane, where he erst had place,
With Corythus did sail to Samothrace;
But now enthronised he sits on high,
In golden palace of the starry sky.


42   BOOK 2, CHAPTER 14.1: Horace, *Odes* 4, 9.25–8.

Many by valour have deserved renown
    Ere Agamemnon, yet lie all oppressed
Under long night, unwept for and unknown;
    For with no sacred poet were they blest.


43   BOOK 2, CHAPTER 21.6: Horace, *Odes* 3, 4.45–8

Who rules the duller earth, the wind-swollen streams,
The civil cities and the infernal realms,

Who the host of heaven and the mortal band
Alone doth govern by his just command.

### 44  BOOK 2, CHAPTER 22.6: Ausonius, *Epigram* 118

I am that Dido which thou here dost see,
Cunningly framed in beauteous imagery.
Like this I was, but had not such a soul
As Maro feigned, incestuous and foul.
Aeneas never with his Trojan host
Beheld my face, or landed on this coast.
But flying proud Iarbas' villainy –
Not moved by furious love, or jealousy –
I did, with weapon chaste, to save my fame,
Make way for death untimely ere it came.
This was my end. But first I built a town,
Revenged my husband's death, lived with renown.
Why didst thou stir up Virgil, envious Muse,
Falsely my name and honour to abuse?
Readers, believe historians; not those
Which to the world Jove's thefts and vice expose.
Poets are liars; and for verses' sake,
Will make the gods of human crimes partake.

### 46  BOOK 2, CHAPTER 23, 4: Horace, *Odes* 3, 24. 36–41

Nor southern heart nor northern snow,
That freezing to the ground doth grow,
The subject regions can fence,
And keep the greedy merchant thence.
The subtle shipmen way will find,
Storm never so the seas with wind.

### 47  BOOK 2, CHAPTER 24.5: Juvenal, *Satires* 8.272–5

Yet, though thou fetch thy pedigree so far,
Thy first progenitor, whoever he were,
Some shepherd was; or else – that I'll forbear.

48  BOOK 3, CHAPTER 7.5: Horace, *Odes* 3, 2. 31–2

Seldom the villain, though much haste he make,
Lame-footed vengeance fails to overtake.


49  BOOK 4, CHAPTER 2.8: Homer, *Odyssey* 18.135–6

The minds of men are ever so affected
As by God's will they daily are directed.


50  BOOK 5, CHAPTER 6.12: Juvenal, *Satires* 10.96–7

Even they that have no murderous will
Would have it in their power to kill.

## 40  Even Such is Time, Which Takes in Trust

Even such is time, which takes in trust
Our youth, our joys and all we have,
And pays us but with age and dust;
Who in the dark and silent grave
When we have wandered all our ways
Shuts up the story of our days.
   And from which earth and grave and dust
   The Lord shall raise me up, I trust.

II EXCHANGES AND RIPOSTES: POEMS
BY QUEEN ELIZABETH, BEN JONSON,
CHRISTOPHER MARLOWE, EDMUND
SPENSER, PHILIP SIDNEY AND OTHERS

41 EDMUND SPENSER:
### To the Right Noble and Valorous Knight, Sir Walter Ralegh

(printed with the first three books of *The Faerie Queene* in 1590)

To thee, that art the summer's nightingale,
Thy sovereign Goddess's most dear delight,
Why do I send this rustic madrigal,
That may thy tuneful ear unseason quite?
Thou only fit this argument to write,
In whose high thoughts pleasure hath built her bower,
And dainty love learned sweetly to indite.
My rhymes I know unsavoury and sour,
To taste the streams that, like a golden shower,
Flow from thy fruitful head, of thy love's praise;
Fitter, perhaps, to thunder martial stower,
When so thee list thy lofty Muse to raise:
    Yet, till that thou thy poem wilt make known,
    Let thy fair Cynthia's praises be thus rudely shown.

## The Passionate Shepherd to His Love

[Answered by No. 22]

Come live with me and be my love
And we will all the pleasures prove
That vallies, groves, hills and fields,
Woods or steepy mountains yields.

And we will sit upon the rocks,
Seeing the shepherds feed their flocks
By shallow rivers to whose falls
Melodious birds sing madrigals.

And I will make thee beds of roses
And a thousand fragrant posies
A cap of flowers, and a kirtle
Embroidered all with leaves of myrtle;

A gown made of the finest wool
Which from our pretty lambs we pull;
Fair lined slippers for the cold,
With buckles of the purest gold;

A belt of straw and ivy buds
With coral clasps and amber studs;
And if these pleasures may thee move.
Come live with me and be my love.

## 43 QUEEN ELIZABETH: On Monsieur's Departure

I grieve, and dare not show my discontent;
I love, and yet am forced to seem to hate.
I do, yet dare not say I ever meant;
I seem stark mute but inwardly do prate.
    I am and not, I freeze and yet am burned
    Since from myself another self I turned.

My care is like my shadow in the sun,
Follows me flying, flies when I pursue it,
Stands and lies by me, doth what I have done.
His too familiar care doth make me rue it.
    No means I find to rid him from my breast,
    Till by the end of things it be suppressed.

Some gentler passion slide into my mind,
For I am soft and made of melting snow;
Or be more cruel, Love, and so be kind;
Let me or float or sink, be high or low.
    Or let me live with some more sweet content,
    Or die and so forget what love ever meant.

## Ah Silly Pug, Wert Thou so Sore Afraid?

[An answer to No. 20]

Ah, silly pug, wert thou so sore afraid?
Mourn not, my Wat, nor be thou so dismayed;
It passeth fickle Fortune's power and skill
To force my heart to think thee any ill.

No fortune base, thou sayest, shall alter thee;
And may so blind a wretch then conquer me?
No, no, my pug, though Fortune were not blind,
Assure thyself she could not rule my mind.

Ne choose I thee by foolish Fortune's rede,
Ne can she make me alter with such speed;
But must thou needs sour Sorrow's servant be,
If that to try thy mistress jest with thee.

Fortune, I grant, doth sometimes conquer kings,
And rules and reigns on earth and earthly things,
But never think that Fortune can bear sway
If Virtue watch and will her not obey.

Pluck up thy heart, suppress thy brackish tears,
Torment thee not, but put away thy fears;
Thy love, thy joy – she loves no worthless bands,
Much less to be in reeling Fortune's hands.

Dead to all joys and living unto woe,
Slain quite by her that never gave wise man blow,
Revive again and live without all dread.
The less afraid, the better thou shalt speed.

## 45  QUEEN ELIZABETH:
### A Hapless Kind of Life Is This I Wear

[Answered by No. 63]

A hapless kind of life is this I wear;
Much watch I dure and weary toiling days.
I serve the rout and all their follies bear,
I suffer pride and sup full hard assays.
To others' will my life is all addressed
And no way so as might content me best.

## The Doubt of Future Foes Exiles My Present Joy

The doubt of future foes exiles my present joy,
And wit warns me to shun such snares as threaten mine
    annoy,
For falsehood now doth flow, and subjects' faith doth ebb,
Which should not be if Reason ruled or Wisdom weaved
    the web.
But clouds of joy untried do cloak aspiring minds,
Which turn to rain of late repent by changed course of
    winds.
The top of hope supposed, the root upreared shall be,
And fruitless all their grafted guile, as shortly ye shall see.
The dazzled eyes with pride, which great Ambition blinds,
Shall be unsealed by worthy wights whose foresight
    falsehood finds.
The daughter of Debate that discord aye doth sow
Shall reap no gain where former rule still peace hath taught
    to know.
No foreign banished wight shall anchor in this port.
Our realm brooks not seditious sects; let them elsewhere
    resort.
My rusty sword through rest shall first his edge employ
To poll their tops that seek such change or gape for future joy.

## 47 QUEEN ELIZABETH (attrib.): Now Leave and Let Me Rest

Now leave and let me rest,
Dame Pleasure, be content;
Go choose among the best,
My doting days be spent.
By sundry signs I see
The proffers are but vain,
And Wisdom warneth me
That Pleasure asketh pain.

And Nature that doth know
How time her steps doth try
Gives place to painful woe
And bids me learn to die,
Since all fair earthly things
Soon ripe will soon be rot,
And all that pleasant springs
Soon withered, soon forgot.

And youth that yields new joys
That wanton lust desires
In age repents the toys
That reckless youth requires;
All which delights I leave
To such as folly trains
By pleasure to deceive
Till they do feel the pains.

And from vain pleasures past
I fly and fain would know
The happy life at last
Whereto I hope to go,
For words or wise reports
Or yet examples gone

Can bridle youthful sports
Till age comes stealing on.

The pleasant courtly games
That I delighted in,
Mine elder age now shames
Such follies to begin,
And all the fancies strange
That fond delight brought forth
I do intend to change
And count them nothing worth.

For I by process worn
Am taught to know the skill,
What might have been forborne
In my young reckless will,
By which good proof I fleet
From will to wit again,
In hope to set my feet
In surety to remain.

## 48 ROBERT DEVEREUX, EARL OF ESSEX:
### Change Thy Mind since She Doth Change

Change thy mind since she doth change,
Let not Fancy still abuse thee;
Thy untruth cannot seem strange
When her falsehood doth excuse thee.
  Love is dead and thou art free;
  She doth live but dead to thee.

Whilst she loved thee best a while,
See how she hath still delayed thee,
Using shows for to beguile
Those vain hopes that have betrayed thee.
  Now thou sees, although too late,
  Love loves truth, which women hate.

Love no more since she is gone:
She is gone and loves another.
Being once deceived by one,
Leave her love but love none other.
  She was false, bid her adieu;
  She was best but yet untrue.

Love, farewell, more dear to me
Than my life which thou preservest;
Life, all joys are gone from thee,
Others have what thou deservest.
  O my death doth spring from hence;
  I must die for her offence.

Die, but yet before thou die
Make her know what she hath gotten;
She in whom my hopes did lie
Now is changed, I quite forgotten.
  She is changed but changed base,
  Baser in so vile a place.

ROBERT DEVEREUX, EARL OF ESSEX (attrib.):
## Go, Echo of the Mind, a Careless Truth Protest

[An answer to No. 3]

Go, echo of the mind, a careless truth protest,
Make answer that so raw a lie no stomach can digest.
For why? The lie's descent is over-base to tell;
To us it came from Italy, to them it came from Hell.
What reason proves, confess; what slander saith, deny;
Let no untruth with triumph pass – but never give the lie.
Confess in glittering court all are not gold that shine,
Yet say one pearl and much fine gold grows in that princely
    mine.
Confess that many tares do overgrow the ground,
Yet say within the field of God good corn is to be found.
Confess some judge unjust the widow's right delay,
Yet say there are some Samuels that never say her nay.
Admit some man of state do pitch his thoughts too high;
Is that a rule for all the rest their loyal hearts to try?
Your wits are in the wane, your autumn in the bud,
You argue from particulars, your reason is not good.
And still that men may see less reason to commend you,
I marvel most amongst the rest how schools and arts
    offend you.
But why pursue I thus the weightless words of the wind?
The more the crab doth seek to creep, the more she is behind.
In church and commonwealth, in court and country both,
What, nothing good, but all so bad that every man doth
    loathe?
The further that you range your error is the wider;
The bee sometimes doth honey suck, but sure you are a spider.
And so my counsel is, for that you want a name,
To seek some corner in the dark to hide yourself from shame.
There wrap the silly fly within your spiteful web –

Both church and court may want you well, they are at no
   such ebb.
As quarrels once begun are not so quickly ended,
So many faults may soon be found but not so soon amended.
And when you come again to give the world the lie
I pray you tell them how to live and teach them how to die.

## When Wert Thou Born, Desire?

When wert thou born, Desire?
    In pomp and prime of May.
By whom, sweet boy, wert thou begot?
    By Good Conceit, men say.
Tell me who was thy nurse?
    Fresh Youth in sugared joy.
What was thy meat and daily food?
    Sad sighs with great annoy.
What hadst thou then to drink?
    Unfeigned lover's tears.
What cradle wert thou rocked in?
    In hope devoid of fears.
What brought thee then asleep?
    Sweet speech, that liked me best.
And where is now thy dwelling-place?
    In gentle hearts I rest.
Doth company displease?
    It doth in many a one.
Where would Desire then choose to be?
    He likes to muse alone.
What feedeth most your sight?
    To gaze on Favour still.
What findest thou most to be thy foe?
    Disdain of my good will.
Will ever age or death
    Bring thee unto decay?
No, no, Desire both lives and dies
    Ten thousand times a day.

## 51 ROBERT DEVEREUX, EARL OF ESSEX:
### Seated between the Old World and the New

Seated between the old world and the new,
A land there is no other land may touch,
Where reigns a queen in peace and honour true.
Stories or fables do describe no such;
Never did Atlas such a burden bear
As she, in holding up the world oppressed,
Supplying with her virtue everywhere
Weakness of friends, errors of servants best.

No nation breeds a warmer blood for war,
And yet she calms them with her majesty;
No age hath ever wit refined so far,
And yet she calms them by her policy.
　　To her thy son must make his sacrifice
　　If he will have the morning of his eyes.

## To Plead My Faith where Faith Hath No Reward

To plead my faith where faith hath no reward.
To move remorse where favour is not borne,
To heap complaints which she doth not regard
Were fruitless, bootless, vain, and yields but scorn.
I loved her whom all the world admired.
I was refused of her that can love none,
And my vain hopes which far too high aspired
Are dead and buried and forever gone
Forget my name since you have scorned my love
And woman-like do not too late lament.
Since for your sake I must all mischief prove.
I none accuse nor nothing do repent.
   I was as fond as ever she was fair,
    Yet loved I not more than I now despair.

## 53 ROBERT DEVEREUX, EARL OF ESSEX:
### Happy Were He Could Finish Forth His Fate

Happy were he could finish forth his fate
   In some unhaunted desert, most obscure
From all societies, from love and hate
   Of worldly folks; then might he sleep secure,
Then wake again and give God ever praise,
   Content with hips and haws and bramble-berry;
In contemplation spending all his days,
   And change of holy thoughts to make him merry;
That, when he dies, his tomb may be a bush,
Where harmless robin dwells with gentle thrush.

## Verses Made by the Earl of Essex in His Trouble

The ways on earth have paths and turnings known.
The ways on sea are gone by needle's light.
The birds of the air the nearest way have flown
And under earth the moles do cast aright.
A way more hard than these I needs must take
Where none can teach nor no man can direct;
Where no man's good for me example makes,
But all men's faults do teach her to suspect.
Her thoughts and mine such disproportion have;
All strength of love is infinite in me,
She useth the advantage time and fortune gave
Of worth and power to get the liberty.
    Earth, sea, heaven, hell are subject unto laws.
    But I, poor I, must suffer and know no cause.

## 55 ROBERT DEVEREUX, EARL OF ESSEX:
### I Am Not as I Seem, I Seem and Am the Same

I am not as I seem, I seem and am the same.
I am as divers deem, but not as others name.
I am not as I should, I should be as I say;
In wanting what I would, I must be as I may.

## I Am Not as I Seem to Be

I am not as I seem to be,
Nor when I smile I am not glad;
A thrall, although you count me free,
I most in mirth most pensive sad.
I smile to shade my bitter spite,
As Hannibal, that saw in sight
His country soil, with Carthage town,
By Roman force defaced down.

And Caesar that presented was
With noble Pompey's princely head
As 'twere some judge to rule the case,
A flood of tears he seemed to shed.
Although indeed it sprung of joy
Yet others thought it was annoy;
Thus contraries be used I find
Of wise to cloak the covert mind.

I Hannibal that smiles for grief,
And let you Caesar's tears suffice:
The one that laughs at his mischief,
The other all for joy that cries.
I smile to see me scorned so,
You weep for joy to see me woe,
And I a heart by love slain dead
Presents in place of Pompey's head.

O cruel hap and hard estate
That forceth me to love my foe,
Accursed by so foul a fate
My choice for to prefix it so,

So long to fight with secret sore
And find no secret salve therefore.
Some purge their pain by plaint, I find.
But I in vain do breathe my wind.

## 57 EDWARD DE VERE, EARL OF OXFORD:
### The Lively Lark Stretched Forth Her Wing

The lively lark stretched forth her wing,
   The messenger of morning bright,
And with her cheerful voice did sing
   The day's approach discharging night.
When that Aurora blushing red
   Descried the guilt of Thetis' bed.

I went abroad to take the air, and in the meads I met a knight,
Clad in carnation colour fair. I did salute this gentle wight,
   Of him I did his name enquire.
   He sighed, and said he was Desire.
Desire I did desire to stay; awhile with him I craved to talk.

The courteous knight said me no nay, but hand in hand with
   me did walk
   Then of Desire I asked again
   What things did please and what did pain.
He smiled, and thus he answered then: 'Desire can have no
   greater pain
Than for to see another man that he desireth to obtain,
   Nor greater joy can be than this,
   That to enjoy that others miss.'

## 58 SIR EDWARD DYER:
## The Shepherd's Conceit of Prometheus

[Answered by No. 59]

Prometheus when first from heaven high
   He brought down fire, 'ere then on earth unseen,
Fond of the light, a satyr, standing by,
   Gave it a kiss, as it like sweet had been.

Feeling forthwith the other's burning power,
   Wood with the smart, with shouts and shriekings shrill,
He sought his ease in river, field and bower,
   But for the time his grief went with him still.

So silly I, with that unwonted sight
   In human shape, an angel from above,
Feeding mine eyes, the impression there did light,
   That since I run and rest as pleaseth love.

The difference is, the satyr's lips, my heart, –
He for a while, I evermore, – have smart.

[An answer to No. 58]

A satyr once did run away for dread,
With sound of horn, which he himself did blow;
Fearing and feared, thus from himself he fled,
    Deeming strange evil in that he did not know.

Such causeless fears when coward minds do take,
    It makes them fly that which they fain would have;
As this poor beast, who did his rest forsake,
    Thinking not why, but how, himself to save.

Even thus mought I, for doubts which I conceive
    Of mine own words, mine own good hap betray;
And thus might I, for fear of maybe, leave
    The sweet pursuit of my desired prey.

Better like I thy satyr, dearest Dyer,
Who burnt his lips to kiss fair shining fire.

60 HENRY NOEL:
## The Foe to the Stomach and the Word of Disgrace

['Raw–Ly'; an answer to No. 35]

The foe to the stomach and the word of disgrace
Shows the gentleman's name with the bold face.

## 61 UNKNOWN:
### If Breath Were Made for Every Man to Buy

If breath were made for every man to buy,
The poor man would not live, rich would not die.

## 62 SIR THOMAS HENEAGE:
### Most Welcome Love, Thou Mortal Foe to Lies

[An answer to No. 18]

Most welcome Love, thou mortal foe to lies,
Thou root of life and ruiner of debate,
An imp of heaven, that troth to virtue ties,
A sun of choice, that bastard lusts doth hate;
A way to fasten fancy most to reason
In all effects, and enemy most to treason;

A flower of faith, that will not fade for smart,
Mother of trust and murderer of our woes,
In Sorrow's sea a cordial to the heart
That medicine gives to every grief that grows;
A school of wit, a nest of sweet conceit,
A piercing eye that finds a gilt deceit;

A fortress sure which reason must defend,
A hopeful toil, a most delighting band,
Affection mazed, that leads to happy end;
To ranging thoughts a gentle reining hand;
A substance such as will not be undone,
A prize of joy for which the wisest run.

## 63 SIR THOMAS HENEAGE:
### Madam, but Mark the Labours of Our Life

[An answer to No. 44]

Madam, but mark the labours of our life
And therewithall what errors we be in;
We sue and seek with prayers, stir and strife
Upon this earth a happy state to win,

And whilst with cares we travail to content us
In vain desires, and set no certain scope,
We reap but things whereof we oft repent us,
And feed our wills with much-beguiling hope.

We pray for honours lapped in Danger's hands,
We strive for riches which we straight forego;
We seek delight that all in poison stands,
And set with pains but seeds of sin and woe.

Then, noble lady, need we not to pray
The Lord of all for better state and stay?

## Sir Henry Lee's Farewell to the Court

His golden locks time hath to silver turned
(O time too swift, O swiftness never ceasing):
His youth against time and age hath ever spurned,
But spurned in vain: youth waneth by increasing.
   Beauty, strength, youth are flowers but fading seen;
   Duty, faith, love are roots and ever green.

His helmet now shall make a hive for bees,
And lover's sonnets turn to holy psalms;
A man-at-arms must now serve on his knees,
And feed on prayers, which are age's alms.
   But though from court to cottage he depart,
   His saint is sure of his unspotted heart.

And when he saddest sits in homely cell,
He'll teach his swains this carol for a song:
'Blest be the hearts that wish my sovereign well,
Cursed be the souls that think her any wrong.'
   Goddess, allow this aged man his right,
   To be your beadsman now that was your knight.

## 65 SIR HENRY LEE:
## Far from Triumphing Court and Wonted Glory

Far from triumphing court and wonted glory,
He dwelt in shady unfrequented places;
Time's prisoner now, he made his pastime story,
Gladly forgets court's erst afforded graces;
That goddess whom he served to heaven is gone,
And he on earth in darkness left to moan.

But lo! a glorious light from his dark Rest
Shone from the place where erst this goddess dwelt,
A light whose beams the world with fruit hath blessed.
Blessed was the knight while he that light beheld;
Since then a star fixed on his head hath shined,
And a saint's image in his heart is shrined.

Ravished with joy, so graced by such a saint,
He quite forgot his cell, and, self denied,
He thought it shame in thankfulness to faint;
Debts due to princes must be duly paid.
Nothing so hateful to a noble mind
As, finding kindness, for to prove unkind.

But ah, poor knight, though thus in dreams he ranged,
Hoping to serve this saint in sort most meet,
Time with his golden locks to silver changed
Hath with age-fetters bound him hands and feet;
'Ay me!' he cries, 'Goddess, my limbs grow faint;
Though I time's prisoner, be you my saint!'

## 66 SIR HENRY WOTTON:
### The Character of a Happy Life

How happy is he born and taught
   That serveth not another's will;
Whose armour is his honest thought,
   And simple truth his utmost skill;

Whose passions not his masters are;
   Whose soul is still prepared for death,
Untied unto the world by care
   Of public fame or private breath;

Who envies none that chance doth raise,
   Nor vice; who never understood
How deepest wounds are given by praise;
   Nor rules of state, but rules of good;

Who hath his life from rumours freed;
   Whose conscience is his strong retreat;
Whose state can neither flatterers feed,
   Nor ruin make oppressors great;

Who God doth late and early pray
   More of his grace than gifts to lend;
And entertains the harmless day
   With a religious book or friend.

This man is freed from servile bands
   Of hope to rise or fear to fall:
Lord of himself, though not of lands,
   And, having nothing, yet hath all.

## 67 SIR HENRY WOTTON:
### On His Mistress, the Queen of Bohemia

You meaner beauties of the night,
   That poorly satisfy our eyes
More by your number than your light,
   You common people of the skies;
What are you when the moon shall rise?

You curious chanters of the wood,
   That warble forth Dame Nature's lays,
Thinking your passions understood
   By your weak accents; what's your praise,
   When Philomel her voice shall raise?

You violets that first appear,
   By your pure purple mantles known
Like the proud virgins of the year,
   As if the spring were all your own;
   What are you when the rose is blown?

## 68  SIR HENRY WOTTON:
### Upon the Sudden Restraint of the Earl of Somerset, then Falling from Favour

Dazzled thus with height of place,
   Whilst our hopes our wits beguile
No man marks the narrow space
   'Twixt a prison and a smile.

Then, since Fortune's favours fade,
   You, that in her arms do sleep,
Learn to swim, and not to wade;
   For the hearts of kings are deep.

But if greatness be so blind
   As to trust in towers of air,
Let it be with goodness lined,
   That at least the fall be fair.

Then, though darkened, you shall say,
   When friends fail and princes frown,
Virtue is the roughest way,
   But proves at night a bed of down.

## 69 SIR HENRY WOTTON: This Hymn

*(Made by Sir H. Wotton, when he was an Ambassador at
Venice, in the Time of a Great Sickness There)*

Eternal mover, whose diffused glory,
    To show our grovelling reason what Thou art,
Unfolds itself in clouds of nature's story,
    Where man, thy proudest creature, acts his part,
Whom yet, alas, I know not why, we call
The world's contracted sum, the little all;

For what are we but lumps of walking clay?
    Why should we swell? whence should our spirits rise?
Are not brute beasts as strong, and birds as gay, –
    Trees longer lived, and creeping things as wise?
Only our souls were left an inward light,
To feel our weakness, and confess Thy might.

Thou then, our strength, Father of life and death,
    To whom our thanks, our vows, ourselves we owe,
From me, thy tenant of this fading breath,
    Accept those lines, which from thy goodness flow;
And Thou, that wert Thy regal Prophet's muse,
Do not Thy praise in weaker strains refuse.

Let these poor notes ascend unto thy throne,
    Where majesty doth sit with mercy crowned,
Where my Redeemer lives, in whom alone
    The errors of my wandering life are drowned;
Where all the Quire of Heaven resound the same,
That only Thine, Thine is the saving name.

Well, then, my soul, joy in the midst of pain;
    Thy Christ, that conquered Hell, shall from above
With greater triumph yet return again,
    And conquer his own Justice with his Love;

Commanding earth and seas to render those
Unto his bliss, for whom he paid his woes.

Now have I done; now are my thoughts at peace;
    And now my joys are stronger than my grief:
I feel those comforts, that shall never cease,
    Future in hope, but present in belief:
Thy words are true, Thy promises are just,
And Thou will find thy dearly bought in dust.

## The Mind of the Frontispiece to Ralegh's *History of the World*

From death and dark oblivion, near the same,
    The mistress of man's life, grave History,
Raising the world to good or evil fame,
    Doth vindicate it to Eternity.

High Providence would so, that nor the good
    Might be defrauded, nor the great secured;
But both might know their ways are understood,
    And the reward and punishment assured.

This makes that, lighted by the beamy hand
    Of Truth, which searcheth the most hidden springs,
And guided by Experience, whose straight wand
    Doth mete, whose line doth sound, the depth of things,

She cheerfully supporteth what she rears,
    Assisted by no strengths but are her own;
Some note of which each varied pillar bears,
    By which, as proper titles, she is known –

Time's Witness, Herald of Antiquity,
The Light of Truth, and Life of Memory.

# The Poets

Poems 1–40  SIR WALTER RALEGH, *c.*1553–1618: soldier,
courtier, explorer, poet. Executed by James I for treason.

41  EDMUND SPENSER, *c.*1552–99: poet. Poet Laureate from
1590 (on publication of first three books of *The Faerie
Queene*). Sometime soldier, governor in Ireland, courtier.
In 1598 his North Cork castle was burned. Next year he
died in London, allegedly in penury. The poets carrying
his coffin threw pens and poems into his grave, with tears.

42  CHRISTOPHER MARLOWE, 1564–93: poet, dramatist.
Murdered, allegedly for political reasons.

43–7  QUEEN ELIZABETH, 1533–1603: monarch from 1558 until
her death.

48–55  ROBERT DEVEREUX, EARL OF ESSEX, 1566–1601:
soldier, courtier. Executed by Elizabeth for treason.

56–7  EDWARD DE VERE, EARL OF OXFORD, 1550–1604:
courtier, soldier, theatre patron.

58  SIR EDWARD DYER, 1543–1607: courtier, diplomat.

59  SIR PHILIP SIDNEY, 1554–86: poet, courtier, soldier;
dedicatee of Spenser's *Shepherd's Calendar*. With Robert
Devereux and Robert Dudley, fought at Zutphen in the
Netherlands (where the English helped the Protestant
Dutch against their Spanish rulers); was wounded in a
cavalry charge and died of his wound. Memorialised in
Spenser's *Astrophel*, elegised by Ralegh in Poem No. 20.

60  HENRY NOEL, *d.*1597: courtier. A Gentleman Pensioner
(member of the sovereign's bodyguard), described
by John Harington as 'one of the greatest gallants' at
Elizabeth's court.

62–3  SIR THOMAS HENEAGE, courtier, *c.*1532–95. Possibly
took over one wing of the secret service at Sir Francis
Walsingham's death, 1590. Briefly considered possible
suitor for Elizabeth. Published his poems in a volume
which included poems by Ralegh and others.

64–5  SIR HENRY LEE, 1533–1611: courtier.

66–9  SIR HENRY WOTTON, 1568–1639: diplomat, friend of
      John Donne at Oxford and secret agent for the Earl of
      Essex. Within sixteen hours of Essex's arrest by Elizabeth
      he was in France. Stayed in Italy till Elizabeth died. After
      James's accession, Ambassador to Venice.

70   BEN JONSON, 1572–1637: poet, dramatist, sometime
     bricklayer, soldier, actor. Jailed several times, once for killing
     another actor in a duel. He pleaded guilty but was released
     (by benefit of clergy) for reciting a Bible verse in Latin.